Two Great Tips for Rea... KT-381-851

* My Great-Aunt Neil, that is.

There are some things <u>no one</u> likes to admit. 1) Pretending the examiners are <u>thick</u> is a great tip. 2) Writing <u>properly</u> gets you more marks. 3) <u>Neil Armstrong</u> was a woman.*

Pretend the Examiners are Thick

This sounds bizarre, but it's actually a <u>really good tip</u>.

Imagine that you have to <u>explain everything</u> to them because they don't understand anything.

I'm thick. Does that mean I'm an examiner?

No!

This goes back to the point about stating the obvious. If you don't make the really <u>simple</u> points, the examiner might <u>not know</u> that you <u>have</u> thought about them.

There's nothing worse than making a fabulously clever point and losing out on marks because the examiner <u>doesn't</u> quite <u>understand</u> what you're getting at.

Make sure what you write is easy to <u>understand</u>.

I wouldn't try anything like this if I were you...

The writer has made Lee a metaphor for the primeval fear which resides in all human kind. The writer identifies his fears with the physical sensation of shivering, giving him a universal, almost Christ-like humanity and calling on our deepest wellsprings of sympathy and self-awareness.

It Doesn't Hurt to Write Properly

You don't get any marks for handwriting. But if the Examiner's just looked at <u>300</u> disgustingly <u>untidy answers</u> and yours is the <u>first nice neat one</u> that hits their eyes, they're going to like you. You bet they are.

Writing in <u>proper sentences</u> with proper <u>punctuation</u> will make it easier for the examiner to understand the points you're making. Make sure you use the right punctuation for <u>quoting</u> — see <u>Section 3</u> for how to do it properly.

Split your answer into <u>paragraphs</u>, one for each of your main points. It'll make it crystal clear to the examiners that you've made lots of <u>separate points</u> and you deserve <u>lots of marks</u>.

Thick examiners — about eight inches across...

Horrible messy writing not proper sentence understand hard very. And remember the poor examiner, struggling to understand even the simplest points. Give them a little <u>glimmer</u> of understanding.

Short Reading Questions

Most of the questions on the Reading paper are itsy-bitsy <u>short</u> ones.
No yellow-polka-dot-bikinis though.

The Short Questions Don't Look Too Bad

1) Some of the short questions are really <u>easy</u>.
2) But some of them need you to do a bit of <u>thinking</u>.
3) Read <u>each question</u> a couple of times before you try answering it so you don't muck up.

Some Questions Check You Understand

Lick your lips if you understand

These questions are testing that you <u>understand</u> what you've read.
They're not that hard, so don't make a <u>big deal</u> out of them.

From paragraph 3, write down how long the Headless Horseman has been living at the inn.

They could ask you to <u>find bits</u> from the writing and <u>write them down</u>.

From the fifth paragraph, give three ways in which goblins are different from trolls.

They could ask you to <u>sum up</u> part of the writing.

Most Short Questions Ask You About the Style

Most of the short questions ask about <u>the way things are written</u>.

Explain how the first paragraph sets a **gloomy** tone.

The trick with style questions is to look at the <u>detail</u>.
Look at <u>each word</u> and decide what it's doing there.

Darn shaving cuts

Mention any gloomy <u>words</u> in your answer.

The hooded man reined in his horse, and wiped the blood from his face. He strained his eyes and ears for a sign that he was nearing safety, but the black night suffocated all sight and sound.

Write about what's <u>happening</u> too. It tells you the man's in trouble and that <u>adds</u> to the gloominess.

<u>Everything</u> you need to answer reading questions is there <u>in the texts</u>.
<u>Keep reading</u> until you <u>find</u> the answer. <u>Don't</u> make things up.

Clogs or wellies — it's all a question of style...

The trick with these short questions is not to get <u>cocky</u>. If you assume they're <u>all</u> easy you could make some nasty mistakes. Read each one through a couple of times and you'll be fine.

Working Out What to Do

Here's what you need to look at on every question to be sure you're doing what they want.

They Tell You Where to Find the Answer

The question always tells you where to look for the answer.

> Explain how the final paragraph is an effective ending for the story.

> From paragraph four, write down two reasons why goblins should not be fed soup.

Don't waste time going through the whole piece of writing for each question. Just go straight to the paragraph they tell you to look at.

If the question says "From paragraph 4..." then look at paragraph 4. The answer will be in there somewhere.

Give them What they Ask For

Some questions make life really easy because they tell you what to write.

write down **two phrases**...

 For this you just need to copy two phrases from the piece you've read.

When they say this, be sure to get that quote in your answer — if you forget it you'll lose a mark.

 Support your answer with a **quotation**...

write down **three reasons**...

 Be darn sure you give three reasons — not two or four.

Open-ended Questions Are Trickier

Some questions don't tell you exactly what to say — you have to work it out.

How does the author *blah*...

Explain **how** the author *blahs*...

 If the question asks how, use by in your answer.
The author creates a spooky atmosphere by...

Explain **why** *blah*...

 If the question asks why, use because in your answer.
The author writes in short sentences because...

For more on this type of question, see P. 20.

Examiners are crazy — paragraph-obsessive...

In nine situations out of ten, the best thing to do is have a slice of cake. If your school doesn't allow cake in the exam hall, you'll have to do the second best thing and get on with the test.

How Much to Write

This page is all about making sure you do <u>just the right amount</u> to get the marks.
Write <u>too much</u> and you're wasting time. Write <u>too little</u>, and you definitely won't get full marks.

Look at the Number of Marks

At the bottom of each question it tells you <u>how many marks</u> you can get for it.
Short questions are worth...

1) For a <u>1 mark</u> question you only need to make one point, find one phrase or give one word.
2) If the question's worth <u>2 marks</u> you'll need to have two bits to your answer.
3) For <u>3 mark</u> questions you'll need to make three points —
    you won't get three marks for a one-word answer.

The Answer Space Shows You How Much to Write

The <u>space</u> for writing the answer gives you a <u>massive clue</u> to how much you should write.

When they give you <u>bullet points</u>, put one point for each.

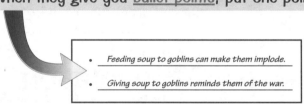

• Feeding soup to goblins can make them implode.

• Giving soup to goblins reminds them of the war.

If the lines go all the way across
the page write a <u>sentence</u>.

• *implosion*

If there's just a small
space write in <u>notes</u>, or
give a <u>one-word answer</u>.

...and one for papa...

For <u>grids</u> it's OK to
write in note form.
Write something in <u>all</u>
the empty boxes.

	Goblins	Trolls
Author's attitude	*thinks they're disgusting*	*admires trolls*
Phrase showing author's attitude	*"fetid stench"*	*"superhuman strength"*

If you can't fit your answer into the space you've written <u>too much</u>.
Read through the question again and check <u>exactly</u> what they wanted.

If your answer <u>hardly</u> fills the space at all something's gone a bit wrong.
You've probably <u>missed something</u> in the piece you had to read. Have <u>another look</u> at it.

Answer space — the final frontier...

This page is easier than falling off a <u>greasy log</u>. Just two simple things you need to remember —
write enough to get the marks, and use <u>all</u> the space they give you for writing your answers.

Mini-Essay Questions

The last question for some texts is a bit <u>longer</u>. You have to do a little <u>mini-essay</u>. Fun, fun, fun.

The Mini-Essay Questions Look Like This

Dashed question must be round here somewhere.

These questions ask about <u>the whole text</u> — don't get stuck in the first couple of paragraphs. Make sure you write about the whole thing.

In the whole text, how does the author mix horror and humour?

You should comment on:
— how the author describes the Goblins
— how the author describes the Trolls
— whether you think there is more horror or humour in the story

(5 marks)

If they give you <u>hints</u>, use them to organise your answer. Write about each one in turn.

You won't <u>always</u> get hints. If you don't, you should still aim to have at least <u>three main chunks</u> to your answer.

You get <u>5 marks</u> for these longer questions. Make one or two points for <u>each</u> of the hints. <u>Back up</u> each point with a <u>quote</u> for full marks.

Don't Spend Ages on the Long Questions

These mini-essays will take a bit <u>longer</u> to do than the shorter questions. Obviously. But you <u>don't</u> have time to muck about.

1) Go back to the piece you've read. Pick out the bits you're going to write about — <u>underline</u> the bits that answer the question, or put <u>stars</u> in the margin.

2) Once you start writing don't do anything fancy. Stick to <u>clear simple English</u>. <u>Make a point</u>, back it up with a <u>quote</u>, and move on to your next point. Keep going till you've made <u>at least</u> 5 decent points.

3) Have a quick read through what you've written to make sure you haven't said anything <u>blatantly stupid</u>.

4) Go on to the <u>next question</u>.

It's over here, dozy butt.

The main thing is not to get <u>bogged down</u>. If you really <u>dry up</u> on one of these questions, leave it. Do all the short questions first, then <u>come back</u> at the end.

Mini-essay — I'd rather have a mini-egg...

These questions are a bit harder than the short questions. But not <u>that</u> much harder. Don't be intimidated by them. Stand up to them. Show the <u>little blighters</u> what you're made of, what-ho.

What Questions Mean

If you want to write a good answer, you'd better make sure that you understand the question.

Work Out What The Question Wants You To Do

Sometimes, the questions aren't quite as straightforward as they might be.
But those hard-looking questions actually just want you to do a few not-so-hard things.

Look at these questions — and see what they really want you to do.

Q. How is suspense created in this story?

① Write about the things that happen in the story.

② Write about the words that the writer uses.

③ Write about the way the story is put together — does the writer leave some things out to make you wonder what's going on?

I feel suspended...

Break it down into easy bits before you try to answer it.

Write about the words the writer chooses to make the castle seem interesting.

Q. In what way does the article make you want to visit the castle?

Say what the writer tells readers about the castle.

Write about the way the writer ends the article — does the writer decide that the castle is worth visiting?

Look out for Key Words in the Question

Work out what kind of question it is. These key words are a massive clue.

Q. How does the writer...

You always have to talk about the words the writer uses and the way the piece is put together for this kind of question.

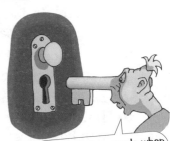

Who needs key words when you've got a key nose...

Q. How does the writer build up a picture of...

Talk about the words the writer uses. If it's a story, talk about the reactions of the narrator and the characters.

Q. What is your impression of the shopkeeper?

Write about what kind of person the shopkeeper is. Say which bits you've used to get your answer.

Different Questions

Different questions need answering in different ways.
It's worth looking out for <u>key words in the question</u> to help you decide how to answer it.

Make Your Answer Fit The Question

1) Different questions can ask about the <u>same thing</u> in <u>different ways</u>.

2) Don't fall into the trap of thinking "This is a question about blurg, so I'll just write about blurg".

3) You really have to look for those <u>key words</u>, and be really <u>sure</u> what the question wants you to do.

Absolutely PUURRRRRfect fit darling....

Both thooo quootions basically mean "write about the supervisor at the doorknob factory" — but you'll get precious <u>extra marks</u> if you tackle them in slightly <u>different</u> ways:

The key words in this question are "<u>What impression</u>".
This is a simple, open question. It's asking you to comment on what the supervisor <u>says and does</u>.

> **Q. What impression do you get of the supervisor at the doorknob factory?**

The key words here are "<u>How does the writer</u>".
This is a bit more specific. You need to write about the writer's <u>use of language</u>.

> **Q. How does the writer make you dislike the supervisor at the doorknob factory?**

You also get a handy <u>hint</u> with this question — the word "<u>dislike</u>".
You know you're looking for things that show the supervisor in a <u>bad</u> light.

How To Make Your Answer Fit The Question

Here's what you might do <u>differently</u> to answer these two questions.
Both answers talk about the <u>same thing</u>, but from slightly <u>different</u> angles.

> **Q. <u>What</u> impression do you get of the supervisor at the doorknob factory?**

> **Q. <u>How</u> does the writer make you dislike the supervisor at the doorknob factory?**

The supervisor of the doorknob factory treats the workers badly. She thinks they are useless, and keeps threatening them with the sack.

The writer spends a long time describing how the supervisor treats her workers. The writer uses words like "yells", "threatened" and "a sarcastic laugh" to show how the supervisor speaks to the workers.

This answer talks about <u>**WHAT**</u> the writer says in the story.

This answer talks about <u>**HOW**</u> the writer says it.

This is about choice of words and structure.

Cabbage Broth *? ? ? Eggs*

Like a chef deciding <u>WHAT</u> to cook.

Fried *? ? Boiled ?*

Like a chef deciding <u>HOW</u> to cook it.

Questions About Language

When they ask questions about the language, you have to write about the <u>words</u> that a writer chooses to <u>describe</u> things. This page shows you what to do, so <u>learn</u> it.

Write about Descriptions

If you're asked <u>how</u> a writer creates a <u>picture</u> of something, you'll have to write about the <u>words</u> that he or she uses to describe it.

> The rustling noise grew louder and more persistent. When it started, Marcie had thought of leaves blowing in the wind, but now it was far too loud for that. It sounded like someone stomping through crisp packets. The rustling turned into crunching, as if some huge animal was munching on a gigantic cream cracker.

The bits in red give you an idea of a really loud crunching sound.

Does the Writer Finish the Description all in One Go?

Often, a writer <u>won't</u> describe the thing they're talking about all in one go. This often happens in stories when a <u>new character</u> or <u>place</u> is introduced to the readers — the writer tells you about them a bit at a time. If you notice this, write about it in your answer. It'll get you <u>more</u> marks.

Write about Words used to Create a Mood

Questions that ask things like "How does the writer <u>build up tension</u>?" look rather nasty. First of all, you need to <u>find words</u> that give you an <u>idea</u> of <u>tension</u> or <u>alarm</u>. Then see how the writer <u>increases</u> the fear and alarm felt by the <u>narrator</u> and the characters in the story.

Her words sure put him in a mood

You big, ugly monster!

Hmmf.

> At first, the narrator is "slightly suspicious" of the man in the green jumper. The writer builds up the narrator's feeling of alarm as she realises that the man is up to no good. She becomes "more and more afraid". The writer describes the narrator's fear when she thinks the man has seen her. This creates tension. The tension is kept up right until the man leaves the museum.

<u>Nothing</u> in the writing is the way it is by <u>accident</u>. The writer has <u>chosen</u> words <u>deliberately</u> to make the readers feel happy, or sad, or tense, or excited or whatever.

Structure

If you're asked about <u>how the writer does something</u> in the story it's always worth writing about how the piece is actually <u>put together</u>. It won't have been written that way by accident.

Are the Beginning and End Different?

You can <u>get</u> <u>asked</u> about this in the Exam, so pay attention.
Sometimes the very <u>end</u> of a piece is written in a slightly <u>different style</u> to create an effect.

Beginning   End

For example, when a writer is trying to <u>persuade</u> readers, he or she might round the piece off by talking in a direct and friendly way about his or her <u>own experience</u>.

Well, I *think* it's different...

<u>Non-fiction</u> articles that <u>start</u> with a question of some sort will <u>end</u> by answering the question. This rounds the article off nicely.

> In conclusion, we can answer the question posed at the beginning of this article by saying that criminals should be rehabilitated as well as punished.

Does the Writer seem to Change his or her Opinion?

Underwater Snooker by Ted Hanson

In the last few years, many bizarre new sports like pogo-stick racing and tree surfing have taken off.
One that seems unlikely to ever become popular is underwater snooker. I must admit, I laughed out loud when the idea was first suggested to me. I couldn't imagine why anyone would want to put on a wetsuit and climb into a swimming pool for a game of snooker.

    I was invited to Sharky's Pool and Snooker Pool, and after a couple of games I was hooked. The experience of potting a ball six feet underwater is something that has to be tried.

It's rubbish!

It's brilliant!

The writer has changed his mind. He's decided he likes underwater snooker.

It <u>isn't</u> that the writer <u>can't</u> make his mind up. He's actually changing his opinion <u>on purpose</u>. He starts off by saying that underwater snooker is crazy — that's something that most readers would <u>agree</u> with. Then he says that <u>he's</u> been <u>convinced</u> by a visit to a snooker pool. He wants readers to <u>agree</u> with him here, too.

Termites love structures — especially wooden ones...

The way that the piece is <u>put together</u> is as important as the <u>words</u> the writer uses for those "how does the writer?" type of questions. Remember — the writer did it that way <u>on purpose</u>.

Questions Asking for Your Opinion

Some questions ask you specifically for <u>what you think</u>.
This is another kind of question that you need to tackle in a <u>slightly different</u> way.

Watch Out For Questions That Want Your Opinion

It's normally a <u>bad idea</u> to write "<u>I think</u>" or "<u>in my opinion</u>" in your reading question answers. The only time you should is if the question specifically asks what you think.

These two questions are very <u>similar</u>, but you'll get more marks for tackling them <u>differently</u>.

The key words are "do you think".

> In what ways does the article try to persuade people to watch more movies?

Write about what the article says <u>and</u> how it says it.

> Do you think the article will persuade people to watch more movies?

With this question you need to write about what the article says and how it says it, <u>AND</u> say <u>how effective</u> you think it is.

This is the way to watch more movies.

How To Answer Opinion Questions

There's no big <u>secret</u> about answering questions that ask what you think. You just have to remember to <u>give reasons</u> for what you think. These can be pretty much the same things you would write to answer a normal question.

> In what ways does the article try to persuade people to watch more movies?

> Do you think the article will persuade people to watch more movies?

The article says that watching movies is a good way to escape from real life for a couple of hours.

You won't escape next time Mr. Pond.

REAL LIFE

I think it will persuade people because everyone needs to forget their troubles for a couple of hours every now and then.

This answer talks about a <u>point</u> the article makes.

This says that <u>you think</u> it's a good point — and it says <u>WHY</u> you think so.

Exams are rubbish — that's my opinion...

Opinion questions are great — you get to say what you think. Just make sure you give <u>reasons</u>, or you'll be throwing marks away. <u>Don't</u> give your opinion unless the question asks you to.

Finding the Important Bits

The hard thing is finding the bit of the writing that tells you the answer to the question.

Find the bits that Answer the Question

> **Q. In what way does the article make readers want to visit the Castle?**

The key to answering questions like this is to find loads of things in the article that help answer the question. Here's the start of the article with the bits you need and the bits you don't need helpfully pointed out...

Callendale Castle, often called one of the finest castles in England, is built on a hill overlooking the village of Callendale in West Bassetshire. On approaching Callendale village, the twin towers of the castle suddenly loomed through the mist, giving the village a mysterious appearance.

Callendale Castle holds many stories, and many secrets. A quick read through the guidebook gave me a colourful insight into the way things must have been inside these forbidding stone walls all those years ago. A secret meeting between King Henry V and a French ambassador took place here during the Hundred Years War. In 1814, the castle narrowly escaped being burnt to the ground when a lazy kitchen boy left a pig roasting on the open fire unattended.

The castle tour took me to a dark, dank dungeon, complete with gruesome instruments of torture. Hidden in one corner is a tiny cell, little more than a hole, where countless prisoners were left to rot away. It is hard to imagine how a grown person could fit into a space so small.

Next, the Armoury Museum conjured up the blood and excitement of a medieval battle. During my visit, a party of schoolchildren were gleefully discussing which of the various gleaming swords they would prefer to have their heads chopped off with — which put me right off my lunch.

You **DON'T** need to say where the castle is.

Mention that it looks mysterious — that makes it sound interesting.

People would want to visit to find out more about the stories and secrets.

You **DON'T** need to retell these stories in your answer. Just say that the writer mentions them.

The writer spends some time talking about the dungeon. People find horrible things fascinating, so this bit is important.

This bit shows the schoolchildren enjoyed visiting the castle.

There'll be a Lot of things that Aren't Important

There'll always be a great load of stuff that's got nothing to do with the question. Don't write about every tiny little thing — only write about the bits that the question asks for.

Panning for gold — pick out the good bits...

Nobody can teach you to pick out the important bits. You have to make sure you go through the text and get all the important bits out. Remember — not all of it will be important.

Question Pointers

This is a <u>massively important</u> page. Face it, losing a whole grade because you didn't <u>read the question properly</u> would be pretty embarrassing. Don't let it happen — <u>learn</u> this page.

Always Use The Question Pointers

Often a question will be followed by some <u>pointers</u> telling you <u>what to put</u> in your <u>answer</u>. Whatever you do, don't ignore these pointers. They're much more than helpful hints from the examiners — they're your ticket to <u>better marks</u>. You'd have to be <u>mad</u> to ignore them.

> **How does the writer try to make you feel sympathy for Mr Hobscuttle?**
> In your answer you should comment on:
> • the way his childhood is described;
> • the way the supervisor at the doorknob factory treats him;
> • the way his relationship with his wife changes.

Write about <u>all</u> of these things.

When it says "you should" it <u>means</u> "you must", and no excuses.

If you write two half-decent paragraphs about <u>each</u> of these three points, you'll get <u>better</u> marks than if you write a brilliant long answer that <u>only</u> talks about <u>one</u> of them.

Write About All of the Points

(1) Don't miss <u>any</u> of the points out. Write about <u>all</u> of them. If you forget to write about one of the points, you will <u>lose marks</u>, and that's <u>guaranteed</u>. Your mark could actually go down a <u>whole level</u> — a <u>seriously hefty</u> drop.

Hey! You forgot to write about me!

• the way his relationship with his wife changes.

Oops.

I felt something drop!

(2) Try to spend a roughly <u>equal</u> amount of <u>time</u> talking about each of the pointers they give you. It doesn't have to be exact, but it shouldn't be far off.

Don't go off the rails — use all the points...

You either learn this or you've had it, basically. When the question says "You should <u>comment</u> on..." it really means "You <u>must</u> write about...". Every year, people lose out on <u>easy marks</u> because they don't <u>follow</u> what the question says. Don't be one of them...

Writing your Answer

You need to know how to <u>put your answer together</u>. Once again, it's all about getting the <u>best possible</u> marks for your answer. So, it looks like you need to get this page <u>learned</u>.

Start by saying How you Answer the Question

It's a <u>good idea</u> to give a little <u>introduction</u> to your answer. All it needs to do is say what your basic answer to the question is. It helps the Examiner to see that you're setting off in the <u>right direction</u>, so it'll help <u>you</u> get <u>more marks</u>.

> This is the <u>basic idea</u> of your answer.

> *The writer makes us feel sympathy for Mr Hobscuttle by describing his life as unhappy. The writer shows us that other people are to blame for Mr Hobscuttle's misfortune.*

Go through All of the Points in Turn

The question pointers actually make it a lot <u>easier</u> to put your answer together. Write about <u>each</u> of the points in turn. It really is that simple.

Through what?

Write about one point...

> *Mr Hobscuttle "always tried in vain" to please his father, which tells us that his father was never happy with anything he did. His parents didn't show him love...*

...and then go on to the next.

> <u>Linking phrases</u> like this show where your answer is <u>going</u>.

> *Another person who treats Mr Hobscuttle badly is the supervisor at the doorknob factory. She...*

POINTS

Make it Obvious that you're Answering the Question

Don't be afraid to be <u>blatant</u> and repeat phrases <u>directly</u> from the <u>question</u>.

It <u>makes</u> the Examiner notice that you've read the question carefully and you're doing your best to <u>answer</u> it.

Of course, you can't just leave it at that — you have to go on and <u>write more</u> about each point.

Only take phrases, not huge chunks, or the Examiner will think you're just copying it from the question and don't know what you're talking about (see P.30).

> *Another area of Mr Hobscuttle's life where the writer tries to make us feel sympathy for him is the way his relationship with his wife changes. For example, the writer says...*

This bit comes from the question.

Chasing the milkman? — I said points, not pints...

It's those good old <u>question pointers</u> again. The idea here is that you use them to <u>help you</u> write a good answer. They're like a ready-made plan. Write about them <u>in order</u>, and there you go, one well-structured answer. See, it's <u>not hard</u>, you just have to <u>remember</u> to do it.

Revision Summary Questions

Way-hey, we made it to the end of the section. There's quite a lot to get to grips with here, and you do need to know it all. There's nothing worse than losing marks because you didn't read the question properly. The best way to make sure you've got everything from this section stored away in that slimey sponge of a brain of yours is to go through the questions on this page over and over again until you're absolutely sure that you know the answers. If you don't, you can go back and check. Remember — the whole point of revision is to find out what you don't know, and then learn it until you do.

1) What are the three Golden Rules about Reading Questions?

2) Toad Girl reckons you shouldn't read the piece of writing first, but should skip straight to the questions. Is she right?

3) Is it okay to say simple, obvious things in your answers?

4) How does pretending the examiners are thick get you better marks?

5) Should you bother being neat?

6) Are questions that ask you what's going on:
   a) easypeasylemonsqueezy
   b) horrendous and not to be attempted
   c) straightforward so long as you read the question carefully?

7) For questions about style is it best to go into lots of detail or be nice and vague?

8) Do short questions tell you where to look for the answer?

9) If the question says "Write down 4 phrases..." should you write down:
   a) up to 4 phrases b) at least 4 phrases c) exactly 4 phrases?

10) Should you normally answer "how" questions with "by" or "because"?

11) Should you normally answer "why" questions with "by" or "because"?

12) If a question's worth 2 marks, how many bits are they expecting in your answer?

13) If you haven't got enough space to write your answer, what should you do?

14) Do the mini-essay questions ask about the odd paragraph, or the whole piece of writing?

15) Do you always get helpful hints on the mini-essay questions?

16) What would be different about your answers to these two questions?
   a) What impressions do you get of the giant mongoose?
   b) How does the writer make you like the giant mongoose?

17) When you get a question about how a piece of writing describes something or makes a picture of something, what do you need to look for so you can give an answer?

18) Is "check if the beginning and end are different"
   a) good advice, b) bad advice, or c) Elvis Presley's middle name?

19) What's the important thing to do for questions that ask you what <u>you think</u> about something?

20) Is it better to write about <u>all</u> the "in your answer you should comment on" points in a question, or to write a whole load about one or two of them?

21) How can you make it obvious that you're answering the question?

Only nine more sections to go...

Ooo, I can't wait...

Example — The Story

Read the <u>story</u> on this page and the next. Go on. It's not that bad.

In this extract, Jerry Derryberry has turned his unsuccessful bakery into a thriving business by selling skateboards for dogs.

Jerry Derryberry was sound asleep when the alarm clock chirped. He was awake in an instant, feeling bright and alert, not like in the old days when he had to struggle to rouse himself from a deep and dreamy slumber.

"Good morning, Kerry," he said cheerfully as he walked into the kitchen, where his wife was busy trying artichokes for breakfast. "Oh no," thought Jerry, "not artichokes again." He'd much rather just have a nice piece of toast. Jerry had been dropping hints for over a week now that he didn't like fried artichokes, but Kerry hadn't noticed. "I'd be quite happy with toast, you know, love."

"*Know Your Vegetables* magazine says the ancient Egyptians considered fried artichokes to be a source of health and strength," Kerry replied humourlessly, bringing two large plates of steaming artichokes to the table. Jerry groaned inwardly. In the past he might have got into an argument with Kerry about her silly magazines, but he was so happy at the success of his shop that he was much more able to cope with her these days.

"Those are bags under your eyes," Kerry said. "You should be sleeping more."

Jerry smiled patiently. "Don't be silly love," he said, "I sleep much more than you do."

Jerry was glad when breakfast was over and it was time to go to work. He positively bounced and skipped the ten minute walk to his shop, so full of energy was he feeling. The door to Jerry's bakery was open, and he could smell the sweet aroma of freshly baking bread. He filled his lungs and beamed with pride to think that this little shop, from which he had struggled to make a living for so long, was now beginning to build him an empire.

"Hello, Wayne," he called. "That smells wonderful. Will you be okay here in the shop while I check on the skateboard factory?"

"Sure thing, boss," Wayne responded. He was delighted to do anything the boss asked, since Jerry had given him that big pay rise.

Jerry closed the shop door behind him and went next door into the factory, which had been a dusty, long-deserted warehouse until he bought it and started manufacturing skateboards for dogs.

Example — The Story

As he closed the factory door behind him and surveyed the dozens of workers busily crafting pooch-sized skateboards, Jerry reflected on how long it had taken him to strike it lucky with one of his inventions. He used to sit at his desk until the early hours of the morning, tired after a long day at work, dreaming up ideas. He'd tried sleeping bags for fish, kangaroo binoculars, jigsaws for gerbils. None had caught on. But finally, he reflected, all those years of enterprise and hard work had paid off.

"What are you working on, Lisa?" he asked his chief designer.

"A new model for poodles," Lisa replied cheerfully. "We have to adapt our other designs because poodles have such small paws."

"Good, good," Jerry smiled benevolently. "Keep up the good work."

Jerry went back into the shop, where Wayne was serving a customer — a big-boned, jolly looking man who had a small, yapping white dog on a leash.

"I'm sorry, sir," Wayne was saying, "but none of our skateboards are suitable for poodles."

The man looked crestfallen. Smoothly, Jerry stepped in to assure him that a new model for poodles was being designed as he spoke. The customer's face brightened and the poodle, perhaps sensing his owner's mood, yapped happily. Jerry spent a moment thinking how wonderful it was that his idea had brought such pleasure into people's lives. Every day he saw customers' smiling faces in his shop, and it always gave him a warm glow of satisfaction.

"That's wonderful," the man said. "Oh, and I'll have a medium-sliced wholemeal loaf while I'm here, please."

Wayne extracted a freshly-baked wholemeal loaf from behind the counter and put it into the slicing machine. Meanwhile, an elderly lady walked in and looked in confusion at the display of dog skateboards lined up on the shelves. Jerry put a considerate arm around her and asked if she needed any help.

"I thought this was a bakery," she said. "I only wanted a nice sticky bun. I'm eighty-seven, you know." Jerry gave her a bun.

"There you are, my dear," he said. "You can have it for free."

From Derryberry's Dream Comes True, by I. O. Silver

... Who says you can't teach an old dog new tricks?

Shorter Questions

Right, you've read the story. The first questions you'll have to answer will be <u>quite short</u>. They put in questions like the ones on this page to test you <u>understand the story</u>.

Showing You Understand the Story

1 The <u>easiest</u> questions of all ask you what's going on.

> From paragraph 6 on page 17 write down how long it took Jerry to walk to work.

Jerry was glad when breakfast was over and it was time to go to work. He positively bounced and skipped the <u>ten minute walk</u> to his shop...

There's the <u>answer</u>.
Stop reading and <u>write it down</u>.
It really is as <u>simple</u> as that.

2 Some questions need a bit more <u>work</u>. You have to <u>explain</u> things from the story.

> From paragraph 1 on page 18, explain why Jerry is happier now than he was in the past.

The paragraph doesn't give the answer in an obvious way. You need to <u>work it out</u>. These are the bits that tell you the answer.

...dozens of workers busily crafting pooch-sized skateboards...

...used to sit at his desk until the early hours of the morning...

For your <u>answer</u> you could write:

> *In the past Jerry used to work hard without getting any results. Now he has dozens of people working for him, putting his ideas into practice.*

The answer <u>doesn't</u> have to be fancy or complicated to get the marks. It just has to be <u>based on the story</u>.

In Non-Fiction Writing You'll Have to Find Facts

You won't always get stories to read. They quite often put in <u>articles</u> from magazines, or <u>leaflets</u> and <u>advertisements</u>. For non-fiction they'll ask you to find <u>facts</u>, e.g.

> From paragraph 3, write down two benefits of seedless jam.

> From paragraph 7, write down one advantage and one disadvantage of selling jam in paper bags.

You answer these in <u>exactly the same way</u> — look at the paragraph, find as many examples as they're asking for, and write them down.

Reading test — name a large town on the Thames...

I'd like to ask the <u>examiners</u> a few questions. Like, why don't you leave us alone... What have we done to deserve this... What have we ever done to you... Do you think this is fair... Why...

Shorter Questions

Here are some <u>more</u> SAT-style questions. These ones are about the style —
they're testing whether you can see what fancy tricks the author's up to.

Go Into Detail on Style Questions

This question <u>sounds</u> vague and general — but that
doesn't mean you can give a <u>wishy-washy</u> answer.

> In the first paragraph, how does the writer show that Jerry enjoys life?

A good answer needs to go into <u>detail</u> about the story.
Read through the paragraph again, looking for <u>individual words</u> that tell you Jerry is happy.

> Jerry Derryberry was sound asleep when the alarm clock <u>chirped</u>. He was
> <u>awake in an instant</u>, feeling <u>bright and alert</u>, not like <u>in the old days</u> when
> he had to <u>struggle</u> to rouse himself from a deep and dreamy slumber.

Then explain how each word or phrase <u>adds</u> to the picture of Jerry as a man who enjoys life.

- *In the first sentence, the writer says the alarm clock "chirped".
  Alarm clocks usually make a horrible noise, and chirping is a
  pleasant sound, so this starts the story off on a positive note.*

  - *Jerry wakes up quickly, feeling "bright and alert".
    This suggests he looks forward to his day.*

  This looks like a lot of writing about just a few words — but you won't get any marks for just putting a one-sentence answer.

- *The writer draws a contrast in the second sentence between the present and the
  past. In "the old days" Jerry had to "struggle" to get out of bed. Now he wakes up
  quickly and happily. This contrast emphasises the idea that Jerry enjoys life now.*

Mistakes People Make on Style Questions

(1) *The writer shows Jerry is happier now than he used to be.* **◄ NO NO NO**

This <u>answer</u> is true enough but it doesn't answer the question.
This person's written <u>about the plot</u> when they should have
been writing about <u>the way the story's written</u>.

(2) *The writer shows Jerry enjoys life by using happy words.* **◄ BAD BAD BAD**

This answer is <u>sort of</u> true too. The trouble is it doesn't go
into enough detail to get the marks. If it quoted some
<u>actual words</u> from the story it would be **WAY** better.

Animal Farm was written in a pig-style...

Don't feel bad if you think this is <u>hard</u>. I think this is hard, and I'm a genius. Really, I am. Go
on, test me. I know my seven times tables and everything. And the <u>meaning of life</u>... *(crazed laughter)*

Mini-Essay Questions

The next four pages are about a <u>longer</u> question.

> **Q3. How does the writer describe Jerry's state of mind?**
>
> In your answer you should comment on:
> — the way Jerry reacts to his wife;
> — how he responds to his workplace;
> — the way he treats his employees;
> — how he reacts to his customers.

Empire State
(of Mind)
Building.

There's loads more that you could write for this one. Luckily, it gives you some <u>pointers</u> so you know which bits to concentrate on.

Before you even start to tackle this question, here are three bits of vitally <u>important</u> advice.

① *Write About All Of Those Pointers*

When it says "you should comment on," it <u>really</u> means "you <u>must</u> talk about".

Those pointers are worth their weight in gold. Read 'em and <u>use</u> 'em.

This question tells you to start off by talking about how Jerry behaves with his <u>wife</u>. Then talk about his <u>workplace</u>. Then his <u>employees</u> and then his <u>customers</u>. Try to write a roughly equal amount about each of them.

Do everything the pointers say and you're guaranteed to get <u>better marks</u>.

② *Think — Why Did The Writer Do It Like This*

Look at the <u>wording</u> of the question. This one starts "how does the writer <u>describe</u>...".

This story isn't just a <u>random</u> collection of thrown together words. It's been <u>deliberately</u> written by a writer who wants you to get something out of it.

When you answer the question, think about what the <u>writer</u> was <u>trying to do</u>.

For example, the writer didn't <u>need</u> to mention anything about Jerry's breakfast. The writer could've <u>skipped it</u> and started talking about Jerry at work. The breakfast scene is only there because the writer <u>thinks</u> it will <u>tell us something</u> about Jerry.

③ *Quote Like You've Never Quoted Before*

Quotes show the examiner you've got your answer <u>from the text</u>, not just made it up on a <u>whim</u>. More importantly <u>good quotes = good marks</u>. See <u>Section 3</u> for more on quoting.

Mini-Essay Questions

With those three bits of vital advice wanging round your head, let's <u>answer</u> the question.

If You See It, Say It — Start with Obvious Points

You have to start by talking about "the way Jerry reacts to his wife". <u>Read</u> that section of the story, and <u>write down points</u> as they occur to you. It doesn't matter if they're obvious.

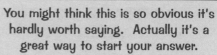

I see SEA

The writer says that Jerry greets his wife "cheerfully". This shows he is in a happy state of mind.

You might think this is so obvious it's hardly worth saying. Actually it's a great way to start your answer.

Starting with an <u>obvious</u> point often makes it easier to think of more <u>subtle</u> ones, like this.

Notice how it <u>links</u> closely to the story and uses two <u>quotes</u>. It also <u>explains</u> what this tells us about Jerry.

Jerry really doesn't want fried artichokes for breakfast — he'd "much rather" have toast. But despite that, he is very polite to his wife. All he says is that he'd be "quite happy" with toast. This shows how kind he is. He doesn't want to hurt her feelings.

Roasted artichoke, marinated in cream and herb sauce and topped with finely toasted croutons, yum. It'll be ready in ten minutes.

Ummm, finely toasted...

Pay Attention To The Writer's Choice Of Words

This question asks you "<u>how does the writer describe...</u>". That makes it especially important to look at what <u>words</u> the writer has <u>chosen</u> to use. One single word can tell you a lot.

Jerry's wife annoys him but he doesn't let it show. He only groans "inwardly" rather than doing it out loud. That shows he's considerate.

Here's a good example of how <u>one word</u> can tell you something important about a character.

I said choice of words, not choice of <u>woods</u>!

The writer <u>doesn't</u> use the word "patiently" by chance. He/she wants to show us that Jerry is generally a patient kind of guy.

The writer says that Jerry smiles "patiently". That shows that Jerry is patient with his wife even though she annoys him.

He calls her "love" twice. This shows how affectionate he is.

Not so obvious, this. Remember that the <u>words</u> people use can be really <u>important</u>.

Mini-Essay Questions

On to pointer number two (see p21): "– how he responds to his workplace".

Huge tackle there on the Pittsburg Pointers.

Tackle The Pointers One At A Time

About the last two-thirds of the story is about Jerry in his <u>workplace</u>. But the third and fourth pointers are about the employees and customers. Don't talk about them just yet — it makes it easier to <u>structure</u> your work if you talk about the pointers <u>one at a time</u>.

Here, we're just looking for <u>descriptions</u> of how Jerry reacts to the workplace itself.

Bit from the story:

He positively bounced and skipped the ten minute walk to his shop, so full of energy was he feeling.

You could write this:

Jerry is very keen to get to work — he "positively bounced and skipped". This shows how much he likes going to work.

Bit from the story:

The door to Jerry's bakery was open, and he could smell the sweet aroma of freshly baking bread. He filled his lungs and beamed with pride...

You could write this:

Jerry "beamed with pride" when he gets to his shop. This shows how proud and happy he is with the shop's success.

You could write this:

Looking at his factory, Jerry thinks about how "all those years of enterprise and hard work had paid off". His state of mind here is that he's pleased with his achievements.

Bit from the story:

As he closed the factory door behind him and surveyed the dozens of workers ... finally, he reflected, all those years of enterprise and hard work had paid off.

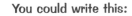

You Can Give Mini-Overviews For The Pointers

It's a good idea to give a short <u>overview</u> for each individual pointer. You could start answering the next pointer ("– the way he treats his employees") like this:

Jerry's state of mind is also revealed by the considerate way in which he treats his employees.

Watch out mate — you've got a mini-over-you.

Then you can go on to make specific points about Jerry and his employees.

Writing a <u>linking</u> sentence like this is a <u>clever trick</u>. It proves that you're <u>carefully following</u> the question.

Mini-Essay Questions

Now you can move smoothly on to the third pointer: "– the way Jerry treats his employees".

Just Write Things Down As You Find Them

Read the text again looking for bits about Jerry and his employees. When you find one that is relevant to the question, simply write down what occurs to you.

① It says that Jerry had given Wayne "a big pay rise". This shows Jerry is generous and wants to share his success.

Keep quoting from the story and explaining why the quotes are relevant.

② The writer describes Jerry as smiling "benevolently" when he's talking to Lisa. This word means he's full of goodwill.

My bread's got no nose.

How does it smell?

Lovely.

③ Jerry praises his employees. He tells Wayne the bread "smells wonderful", and he says to Lisa "keep up the good work". He's in a good mood and he's pleased with what his workers are doing.

There's No Such Thing As Being Too Obvious

Nearly there — just the last pointer to cover. Now we're looking for examples of what Jerry's reactions to his customers tell us about his state of mind.

I've said it before and I'll say it again — don't be scared to state the obvious.

Every day he saw customers' smiling faces in his shop, and it always gave him a warm glow of satisfaction.

Jerry is pleased that his shop is making other people happy — it gives him "a warm glow of satisfaction".

The writer uses the word "considerate" when Jerry puts his arm round the old woman. This shows he's caring.

PLEASE DO NOT FEED THE ANIMALS

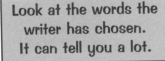

GLOW WORM OF SATISFACTION

Look at the words the writer has chosen. It can tell you a lot.

By giving the old woman a free bun, Jerry again shows his kind and generous state of mind.

Use your fingers — they're handy pointers...

This is a long answer, so there's plenty to learn from it. Always read the handy pointers you get underneath the question, and use them when you go about your answer.

Revision Summary Questions

Da da daa! Revision Summary questions... Alright alright, not the most exciting things, but they ARE the most useful. You can really test your knowledge and make sure you know it all. If there's anything you get stuck on, then go straight back over those pages, and get it learned. Reading test success is all about how you tackle the questions. Pretty obvious really, but that's why this section is so important.

1) How do you find the answers to short questions?
   a) Look in the paragraph where they tell you to look.
   b) Pluck them from thin air.

2) What type of question do you need to pick out individual words for?

3) Writing obvious points in your reading answers will do two of these things. Which ones?
   a) Lose you marks.   b) Help you to think of cleverer points.   c) Nothing at all.
   d) Waste time.   e) Win you marks.   f) Make it snow doughnuts in July.

4) What's the big deal about quoting?

5) When you answer a question, you have to pick out all the relevant bits that are to do with the question. Can you write about other things as well?

6) How can you start your answers?

7) How do you back up your points?

8) When the question has handy pointers underneath, how many of them should you write about?

9) 90% of Columbian fruit bats think that authors just throw words together at random. Are they right? If not, what should your approach to it be?

10) Is it better to talk about the pointers
    a) kind of mixed in together,   b) just one at a time,   or   c) in Latin?
    Why?

11) What happens when you're being too obvious? ← (This is a trick question.)

The 'red ing' test...

Give Reasons

This is a <u>bargain basement</u> of a section — it'll really help your marks on the Reading paper <u>and</u> the Shakespeare question. That's excellent value. And it grates <u>carrots</u> too.

Give Reasons from the bit of Writing

You have to give <u>reasons</u> for what you say — <u>examples</u> from the passage you've read that show where your answer comes from.

If you <u>don't</u> give reasons, the examiners can't tell if <u>you know</u> what you're talking about. Examples show you haven't got it right by a lucky fluke.

> *The women at the banjo club aren't very friendly. In fact they're downright rude.*

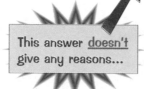
This answer <u>doesn't</u> give any reasons...

...but this answer gives a <u>reason</u> from the writing to justify every point it makes. That's loads better.

> *The women at the banjo club aren't very friendly — they ignore Mrs Icenoggle when she tries to say hello. In fact they're downright rude — they look at her, but then they start talking among themselves.*

Every Time you make a Point — give an Example

It's easy to <u>forget</u> to give examples from the bit of writing you've read. You'd think because the examiner <u>knows</u> what you've read, they'd easily get what you're talking about.

But that's the road to <u>losing</u> loads and loads of marks. They <u>want</u> you to refer to the writing — as if they <u>didn't know it</u>. Drum this simple rule into your head:

> <u>Every time</u> you make a <u>point</u>, <u>back it up</u> with an <u>example</u>.

Hey bear — gimme some cover while I'm making this point.

No fear, partner — I'll be your back-up. Those guys don't stand a chance!

Never forget your back-up

Give reasons — and currants, and sultanas...

The <u>sure-fire</u> way to get good marks in these English SATs is to make sure you put loads of <u>examples</u> in your answer. <u>Reasons</u> and <u>examples</u> — <u>nothing else</u> is going to do.

Using your Own Words

When you link your answer to the piece you've read, use <u>new words</u> to show you understand it.

Don't just Copy Bits Out

When you give your answer, <u>don't</u> just <u>copy out</u> what the piece says word for word.
Any old fool can do that, so it <u>doesn't prove</u> to the examiner that you've <u>understood</u> it.

Here's part of a story:

> "Hello," Mrs Icenoggle began to say. But the sour-faced woman turned away and started to talk to her companions.

When Mrs Icenoggle began to say hello, the sour-faced woman turned away and started to talk to her companions.

No stealing the words straight from the text.

This isn't a good way to talk about the story.

It uses all the <u>same words</u> as the story — it <u>doesn't</u> show that you <u>understand</u>.

Don't be a Copy cat

Put your Reason In Your Own Words

Prove you've understood what you've read — use <u>your own words</u>.

Banjo Club

Hello.....Hello.....

I wonder what's goat into them?

The woman ignored Mrs Icenoggle when she tried to say hello.

All I've done here is say what happened <u>in my own words</u> — but it proves I know what's going on.

Be careful you don't get confused between <u>referring</u> to a story and <u>quoting</u> from it.
Quoting means <u>copying bits out</u> word for word and putting <u>speech marks</u> round them.
There's more on quoting on the next page.

Remember — when you're giving a reason <u>always use your own words</u>.

Tracing teeth marks? — don't copy 'bites' out...

You know you have to <u>give reasons</u> and <u>explanations</u> in your answer and that means you've gotta <u>use your own words</u>. So kick-start your brain and say it <u>your way</u> — don't just copy it.

How to Quote

You can make plenty of good points in your answer, but you won't get all the marks if you don't stick in loads of <u>lovely quotes</u> too.

Quote, Quote, Quote — And Quote Some More

Examiners <u>love</u> you to quote bits from the writing. It'll get you <u>masses</u> of extra marks.

Quotes are great because they show <u>exactly</u> which bit you've got your answer from.

Quoting <u>isn't</u> the same as stealing words from the story or article you've read. There's a <u>massive difference</u>...

Quotes Have Speech Marks

<u>Speech marks</u> make all the difference. They show that <u>you're quoting</u>, not just stealing words. Without speech marks you'll lose marks.

 66 Everything inside the speech marks is a quote. It has to be word for word what the text says. **99**

> "Hello," Mrs Icenoggle began to say. But the sour-faced woman turned away and started to talk to her companions.
> "Did you go to Iona's party last weekend?" she asked.
> All the other women glanced briefly at Mrs Icenoggle. "I certainly did," replied one of them, "and I don't like the way Iona has redecorated her toilet."
> Mrs Icenoggle, who had no idea who Iona was, stood helplessly by the doorway...

The writer describes one of the women as "sour-faced" That makes us think she's not a nice person.

Speech Marks

The <u>speech marks</u> show that you're <u>quoting</u>. When you quote, make sure it's copied <u>word for word</u>.

The women at the banjo club are rude. They talk among themselves even though they all know Mrs Icenoggle is there — "all the other women glanced briefly at Mrs Icenoggle".

Speech Marks

Quote early, quote often...

Remember — <u>copying</u> = <u>bad</u>, but <u>quoting</u> = <u>good</u> (sounds daft, I know, but it's true). If you only learn one other thing about quoting, learn this: Quotes always have to have speech marks.

Explain the Quote

It's no good just sticking a quote down on its own. That doesn't prove anything.
You have to make sure you <u>explain why you're using a quote</u>.

 1 <u>You can Put the Explanation Before the Quote</u>

Here I've used a quote to <u>back up a reason</u> I've just given.

> The answer <u>makes a point</u> — it says the women are rude.

> Then there's <u>a reason to back it up</u> — the women talk among themselves even though they know Mrs Icenoggle is there.

> Now there's a quote from the text. The quote <u>proves the point</u> that the other women all know Mrs Icenoggle is there.

The women at the banjo club are rude. They talk among themselves even though they all know Mrs Icenoggle is there — "all three other women glanced briefly at Mrs Icenoggle".

Eggs's pain

> Ouch!
> ↓ this is bloomin hot!

 2 <u>You can Give the Quote First</u>

This is an example of the <u>second</u> kind of way to use a quote.

A rooster laying an egg?
Eggs-plain that one!

The writer describes one of the women as "sour-faced". That makes us think she's not a nice person.

> This time the quote gets in there first.
>
> Then the answer explains why it's relevant to answering the question.

> If I just wrote this bit, I wouldn't get as many marks. The examiner needs to know why you think the quote is important.

The writer describes one of the women as "sour-faced".

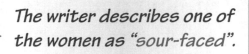 Always <u>explain why</u> the quote is relevant.

It <u>doesn't matter</u> what order you do it in — make a point, then back it up with a quote — or quote then explain. The important thing is that you <u>always explain why</u> your quote helps you <u>answer</u> the question.

<u>*Eggs — plain, fried or scrambled...*</u>

<u>You</u> know why you've chosen your quote. The Examiners <u>won't know</u> — so you need to <u>tell</u> them.

Keeping Quotes Short

<u>Don't</u> think that you'll get better marks for using <u>longer</u> quotes.
You <u>won't</u>. In fact you'll <u>lose</u> marks for it.

Never Quote More than A Few Words...

Quotes are to show that <u>you've read the bit of text</u> you're talking about.
You usually only need to quote a few words.

> Follow the path of few words you must.

Macbeth sees life as a pointless performance —
"Life's but a walking shadow, a poor player
That struts and frets his hour upon the stage
And then is heard no more. It is a tale
Told by an idiot, full of sound and fury,
Signifying nothing." (Act 5, Scene 5, 24-28)

Macbeth sees life as a pointless performance —
"Life's but a walking shadow, a poor player..."
(Act 5, Scene 5, 24)

This quote is <u>far too long</u>. It <u>doesn't</u> make the answer better, and it uses up precious <u>time</u> that you could spend writing something else.

This quote is much better. It's <u>short</u> and it has everything you need to <u>make your point</u>.

Try to quote using the <u>fewest</u> number of words you can. Don't be afraid just to quote a <u>single word</u> if it's <u>enough</u> to make your point.

Far too long!

Short & to the Point

... But Do It Often

Your answer should be <u>full</u> of <u>short</u> quotes <u>backing up</u> your points.

Every time you make a <u>point</u>,
try to <u>find a quote</u>
to back it up.

Hey Pedro,
Do you get my POINT?

You might not always be able to, but <u>always try</u>. Your answers will be much better with loads of <u>good quotes</u>.

Phew-urgh words are better...

You <u>don't</u> need to quote vast chunks of writing, just the bit that makes the point. Be economical.

Revision Summary Questions

Quoting is dead important — "Quote me baby one more time," as Britney Spears once said... Maybe not. Anyhow, there's no way to get all the marks you want, without a clear and thorough understanding of the whole of this section. Test yourself on these questions, and go over the section until you can do them all.

1) What do you have to do to back up every point you make?

2) When you give your answer, is it OK to write your reasons in exactly the same words as the piece of writing uses?

3) If it's not OK, why not? What should you do instead?

4) When can you copy the words exactly?

5) How do you show that something's a quote?

6) Is using quotes   *a)* a bad idea,   *b)* against the law in Stockholm, or   *c)* a great idea?

7) What are the two important ways of giving a reason and explaining it with a quote?

8) What are the rules on how long a quote should be?

9) How often should you use quotes?

What You Have To Do

On the Shakespeare paper you have to answer a question about the <u>set scenes</u> you're doing. This section is full of tips on how to answer the Shakespeare question well. So <u>get stuck in</u>. There are two big things you <u>have</u> to do to get marks.

1) Show You Understand What's Going On

Don't worry — it's not just you who reads Shakespeare and thinks "<u>aargh</u> — what does it <u>mean</u>?"

What's going on?

I'm not sure. That's half the battle.

The <u>examiners</u> know that — and you'll get plenty of marks just for showing that you know what's happening.

To show you <u>understand</u> the bit of the play, you need to:

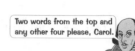
Two words from the top and any other four please, Carol.

1) Write about the way the characters are <u>feeling</u>.
2) Write about Shakespeare's <u>choice of words</u>.

2) Use Quotes To Back Up Your Points

Remember I banged on about how important <u>quoting</u> is in your reading paper — well, it's just as important in the Shakespeare paper — if not more so. You <u>have</u> to quote.

If you talk about the play <u>without</u> using bags of quotes, they won't be convinced that you really <u>know</u> your stuff.

I need help — He's got quotes to back him up.

Make sure you stick your quotes in <u>speech marks</u>, and only use the <u>exact</u> words that Shakespeare uses.

And — You'll Do Better if You Write Well

1) You <u>don't</u> get marks for writing flashy English on the set scenes question. But if you write <u>badly</u> the examiners won't be able to <u>understand</u> what you're saying, and that'll make them <u>grumpy</u> and <u>stingy</u> with marks.

Write well and you'll get a good mark.

2) Don't forget to write in <u>paragraphs</u>. Every time you want to talk about a <u>new idea</u>, start a <u>new paragraph</u>.

3) Here's the <u>tough</u> one — try to sound <u>interested</u> in the play, even if you don't like it. Show the examiners that you're keen by using lots of <u>interesting words</u> and <u>phrases</u> in your answer.

Writer manages to sit — Shakespeare SAT success...

Your three tips for Shakespeare success — show you get what's <u>going on</u>, use lots of <u>quotes</u> from the play, and write <u>clearly</u> in proper <u>paragraphs</u>, with some <u>interesting</u> words. Not much, then...

Shakespeare's Language

It doesn't matter if you think Shakespeare is <u>weird</u> or <u>boring</u>. The important thing is it's <u>not impossible</u>. This section's here to make it all less scary and more doable.

It's Weird — but it gets Easier With Practice

Once you get used to the annoying weird language, Shakespeare is perfectly doable. Remember, you <u>don't</u> have to like it, but you <u>do</u> have to <u>do an Exam</u> on it.

And it's not <u>**THAT**</u> boring. The plays have <u>stories</u> full of <u>violence</u>, <u>villains</u>, <u>murder</u>, <u>love</u>, <u>double-crossing</u> and <u>betrayal</u>.

The key thing about Shakespeare is getting to grips with the <u>funny language</u>. It's not easy, but you can <u>learn</u> how to do it. <u>Practise</u> reading your scenes — the more you read them, the <u>easier</u> they'll be to understand.

You Don't Have To Understand Every Word

That's right — if you read it loads and there are still bits you look at and go "<u>huh</u>?", don't worry. It's OK. As long as you've got the basic <u>idea</u> of what's going on, you'll be fine.

Take a look at this — it's the kind of question you'll get in the exam.

My, my, what a scene.

But I don't understand it.

Imagine you are the Nurse. Write your reactions to the day's events.

This tests if you've <u>understood</u> what <u>happened</u> in the scene, and what the Nurse thought about it. If you show you understand basically <u>what's going on</u>, you <u>don't</u> need to explain the meaning of every single word.

Don't look at your exam paper and have an attack of the <u>wobblies</u> because there's a tiny bit of the <u>scene</u> you don't understand.

You don't need to understand <u>every single word</u>. You need to understand <u>what's going on</u> in the scene you get in the Exam.

Oil gauge, pressure gauge — what's a lan guage...

Shakespeare <u>isn't</u> that boring if you understand the <u>weird language</u>. It gets easier with practice, and in any case you don't have to understand <u>all</u> of it — as long as you get the basic idea.

Tricky Play Terms

You'll just have to <u>learn</u> these words, I'm afraid. Without them it'll never quite make sense.

A Play is divided into Acts and Scenes

The play is divided into <u>five</u> big sections, called <u>acts</u>. Each act is like an <u>episode</u> of a TV serial — lots of things happen in it, but it's only <u>part</u> of the whole thing.

Each act is made up of <u>smaller</u> sections called <u>scenes</u>. Scenes are just a way of <u>breaking up</u> the story. A new scene starts when time has passed or the story moves to a different place.

"Act" and "Scene" are two words you're likely to have to bandy about in the SAT, so make sure you know what they mean.

In the SAT, you'll probably get a question on <u>one whole scene</u> and a <u>bit</u> from <u>another scene</u>.

Shakespeare wrote Three Kinds of Play

Shakespeare wrote <u>three</u> main kinds of play. You can <u>impress</u> the examiner by using these words in your SAT, so make sure you know what they mean.

① TRAGEDIES = People <u>die</u> at the end.

Romeo and Juliet and *Macbeth* are tragedies.

② COMEDIES = People get <u>married</u> at the end.

Twelfth Night and *A Midsummer Night's Dream* are comedies.

③ HISTORIES = These are based on <u>real history</u>.

Henry V and *Julius Caesar* are histories.

Characters are the People in the Play

There are a few <u>main</u> characters in each play that you have to know all about. There are also loads of <u>minor</u> characters who don't do anything very important. For example, in Julius Caesar:

These three are important characters

The <u>other</u> conspirators <u>aren't</u> that important.

Antony   Brutus   Cassius

Burn the people in the play — Char-actors...

Seems a bit like a list of random facts about Shakespeare's plays to me. They are <u>important</u> random facts, though. Don't let yourself get <u>acts</u> and <u>scenes</u> mixed up, and remember those <u>three types</u> of play. You'll be able to impress the examiner with them, and that means a better grade.

More Play Features

A lot of the things you'll find <u>odd</u> when you read a scene from Shakespeare are there because it's a <u>play</u>. Learn what it all means now and you won't be <u>confused</u> in the Exam.

Plays are written to be Acted

This is a <u>massive</u>, <u>huge difference</u> between a Shakespeare play and a novel or short story. A novel tells a story by <u>describing</u> it to you. A play tells a story by <u>showing</u> it to you.

You <u>don't</u> get any long describing bits in a play. The actors show the audience what's going on by the <u>way</u> they say their lines — laughing, shouting or whatever — as well as <u>what</u> they say.

The audience <u>don't</u> have the <u>playscript</u> in front of them, so the <u>actors</u> have to do all the <u>work</u>.

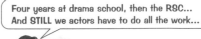

Four years at drama school, then the RSC... And STILL we actors have to do all the work...

In the Exam, <u>you</u> have to do all the work. You have to work out what's going on <u>just</u> by reading the scenes.

Sometimes Characters Talk To Themselves

Talking to yourself — crazy.

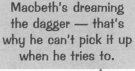

This seems <u>strange</u>. People in real life don't <u>usually</u> talk to themselves — if they did, pretty soon you'd start to <u>worry</u> about them.

Characters in plays do this so the audience can hear what they're <u>thinking</u> and <u>feeling</u>. They're really talking for the <u>benefit</u> of the audience.

MACBETH   Go bid thy mistress, when my drink is ready,
                She strike upon the bell. Get thee to bed.

[*Exit* SERVANT]

Is this a dagger which I see before me,
The handle toward my hand? Come let me clutch thee: —
I have thee not, and yet I see thee still.

> Macbeth's dreaming the dagger — that's why he can't pick it up when he tries to.

> The servant has gone. Macbeth is on his own.

Macbeth is <u>thinking</u> these things. People don't usually think out loud, but you wouldn't know what was going on in Macbeth's head if he didn't <u>tell</u> you. Shakespeare makes him say it <u>out loud</u>.

Is this a badger which I see before me?

Sometimes characters say thoughts <u>aloud</u> when <u>other</u> characters are on the stage. When you see the word [Aside], that's what's happening — the <u>audience</u> can hear, but the <u>other</u> characters can't.

Plays for insects — written to bee acted...

It seems pretty <u>weird</u> to me. They were all written to be <u>acted on stage</u>, but you have to read them — there's no one to <u>act it out</u> in the Exam, so you have to understand it all from the <u>script</u>.

More Play Features

When you <u>read</u> Shakespeare plays, it helps if you <u>imagine</u> what would be happening if they were being said by <u>actors</u> on stage. Luckily, you get some <u>clues</u> as to what would be going on.

Stage Directions Give a Few Clues

Stage directions show the actors what to do, when to come in and when to leave the stage.

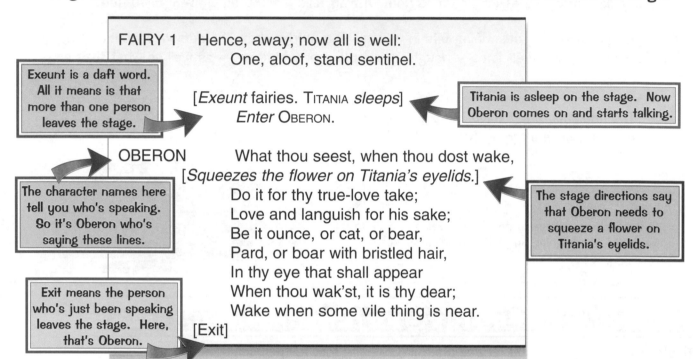

FAIRY 1   Hence, away; now all is well:
              One, aloof, stand sentinel.

[*Exeunt* fairies. TITANIA *sleeps*]
    Enter OBERON.

OBERON   What thou seest, when thou dost wake,
[*Squeezes the flower on Titania's eyelids.*]
    Do it for thy true-love take;
    Love and languish for his sake;
    Be it ounce, or cat, or bear,
    Pard, or boar with bristled hair,
    In thy eye that shall appear
    When thou wak'st, it is thy dear;
    Wake when some vile thing is near.
[Exit]

Callout: Exeunt is a daft word. All it means is that more than one person leaves the stage.

Callout: Titania is asleep on the stage. Now Oberon comes on and starts talking.

Callout: The character names here tell you who's speaking. So it's Oberon who's saying these lines.

Callout: The stage directions say that Oberon needs to squeeze a flower on Titania's eyelids.

Callout: Exit means the person who's just been speaking leaves the stage. Here, that's Oberon.

Stage directions are <u>great</u>, because they tell you the basics of what's <u>happening</u> on stage. Always read them when you read a play.

The Director Decides the Rest

Sometimes the stage directions <u>tell</u> the actors how to say their lines. More often though, the <u>director</u> has to work out how the actors should say the lines — sadly, angrily or whatever.

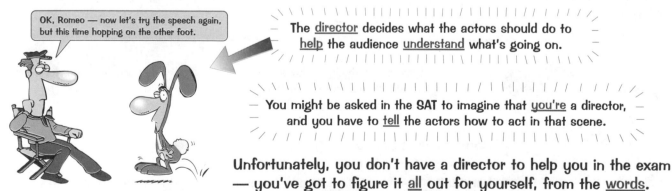

Speech bubble: OK, Romeo — now let's try the speech again, but this time hopping on the other foot.

The <u>director</u> decides what the actors should do to <u>help</u> the audience <u>understand</u> what's going on.

You might be asked in the SAT to imagine that <u>you're</u> a director, and you have to <u>tell</u> the actors how to act in that scene.

Unfortunately, you don't have a director to help you in the exam — you've got to figure it <u>all</u> out for yourself, from the <u>words</u>.

Past the curtains, on your right — stage directions...

Right, so that's what <u>stage directions</u> are, then. Use them to help you imagine how the actors would be <u>saying</u> the words and what they'd be <u>doing</u> on the stage. Don't forget: exeunt = exit.

The Language

When you first read a Shakespeare play, it seems like you'll never <u>understand</u> a word. <u>Don't give up</u>, though. The <u>more</u> you read the play, the <u>easier</u> it gets and the more <u>you'll get it</u>.

The Language Isn't Everyday Modern English

<u>Shakespeare</u> wasn't trying to <u>confuse</u> you by using <u>funny language</u> — believe it or not, when he was alive people <u>really did use</u> those strange words. He wrote his plays <u>about 400 years ago</u>.

See if this speech from _Romeo and Juliet_ is any easier to understand after you've read the "translation".

Juliet is in love with Romeo but she knows she can't marry him because he's Romeo Montague — and Juliet's family don't get on with the Montague family. Here, she's imagining that she is talking to Romeo.

Hi — I'm Trevor.

Here's what Juliet says...

...and this is roughly what it means.

JULIET 'Tis but a name that is my enemy;—
Thou art thyself though, not a Montague.
What's Montague? It is not hand, nor foot,
Nor arm, nor face, nor any other part
Belonging to a man. O, be some other name.

What's in a name? That which we call a rose,
By any other name would smell as sweet;
So Romeo would, were he not Romeo call'd,
Retain the dear perfection which he owes
Without that title:—
          Romeo, doff thy name;
And for that name, which is no part of thee,
Take all myself.

The only problem is your name. But you are you, and "Montague" is just a word. People aren't made up of words, they're made up of hands, feet, arms and faces. I wish you weren't called Montague.

Names aren't important. If roses had another name, they'd still smell nice. It's just the same with Romeo. If he was called something else, he'd still be perfect to me.

Romeo, get rid of your name, and take me instead.

Mmmmmm baby — what did you say your name was again?
Errm, Humphrey.
Well Humph, you sure do smell sweet.

Some Sentences are in a Funny Order

People <u>swapped</u> round the <u>order of words</u> a lot more in those days. If you <u>jiggle</u> the word order around a bit you can usually work out what it means.

Villain am I none
= I am not a villain

Thus with imagined wing our swift scene flies
= Shakespeare is asking the audience to imagine that the scene is moving to another place.

Order! ORDER!
Chortle-chortle!
Teeheeheee!
Ha-ha-ha!
Phnah-phnah-phnah!

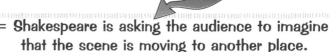
But the witness was as drunk as a judge!
Don't you mean as drunk as a lord?
Yes, my lord.

Funny Sentences — by order of drunken judges...

"But I don't understand a word of it!" I hear you cry. Don't panic. Keep reading it and try to pick out a bit here and there. You only need to know what's going on — not every word.

The Language

Shakespeare writes a lot in <u>verse</u>, or <u>poetry</u> — and he often uses lots of words to say something <u>simple</u>. This page will help you to <u>make sense</u> of what you're reading.

Don't Stop Reading At The End Of The Line

When you read verse, it's <u>tempting to stop</u> at the <u>end</u> of a line. <u>Don't</u> — unless there's a full stop, the sentence carries on. It makes <u>no sense</u> if you <u>pause</u> at the end of every single line. Try reading this extract from *The Tempest*.

ALONSO	You cram these words into mine ears against The stomach of my sense. Would I had never Married my daughter there! For, coming thence, My son is lost; and, in my rate, she too, Who is so far from Italy removed I ne'er again shall see her. O thou mine heir Of Naples and of Milan, what strange fish Hath made his meal on thee?

If you stop at the end of each line, this makes no sense.
It would sound like: "O thou mine heir. Of Naples and of Milan, what strange fish. Hath made his meal on thee?"

It'll make a lot more sense if you read it all as one sentence: "Oh thou mine heir of Naples and Milan, what strange fish hath made his meal on thee?"

Don't pause at the end of lines when you're reading Shakespeare — <u>pause</u> when you get to <u>punctuation</u>, the <u>commas</u> and <u>full stops</u>, like in other writing. It'll make <u>much more sense</u>.

Characters Use An Awful Lot Of Words

One thing you're <u>bound</u> to notice about Shakespeare is that the characters <u>don't half go on</u>. They use an <u>awful lot</u> of words to say something <u>simple</u>.

Have <u>another look</u> at that speech by <u>Alonso</u>, from *The Tempest*. He talks for ages but all he's saying is <u>basically</u> this:

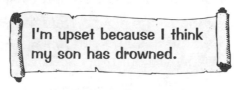

I'm upset because I think my son has drowned.

The way the speeches are so <u>long-winded</u> might be a bit <u>irritating</u>, but it's <u>the key</u> to getting <u>good marks</u>. You have to talk <u>about how</u> Shakespeare uses this <u>flowery language</u> to show what <u>characters</u> are <u>thinking</u> and <u>feeling</u>.

Shakespeare was probably paid by the word...

Make sure that you don't pause at the end of each and every line — look at the <u>punctuation</u> instead. And bear in mind that characters use loads of words for ideas that are basically simple.

The Language

You'd have to be <u>as nutty as a fruitcake</u> to walk around <u>speaking in poetry</u>. I don't do it (much). Understand why Shakespeare wrote like that and you've got a head start in the SAT.

Only The Posh Characters Talk In Poetry

In Shakespeare's day, writers always made their <u>posher</u> characters talk in <u>verse</u> — while the more <u>common</u> characters talked in normal, <u>everyday prose</u> (like, not poetry).

CLAUDIO	Sweet Hero, now thy image doth appear In the rare semblance that I loved it first.
DOGBERRY	Come, bring away the plaintiffs. By this time our sexton hath reformed Signior Leonato of the matter. And, masters, do not forget to specify, when time and place shall serve, that I am an ass.

In this scene from *Much Ado About Nothing*, the lord Claudio talks in verse, but Dogberry (an ordinary man) talks in prose.

If Shakespeare had made Claudio talk in prose, it would have sounded daft to audiences at the time — kinda like a BBC newsreader talking in cockney slang.

<u>Posh characters</u> talk in <u>fancy poetry</u>. Sometimes poorer characters talk in verse too, but usually only when they're spouting about big ideas.

<u>Sometimes</u> the posher characters talk in <u>prose</u> — like Pedro, Claudio and Benedick in Act V, Scene 1. Urgh — confusing. It doesn't mean they've suddenly become lower class — it means they're bantering with each other in a casual, chummy way.

Some Posh Spices

Poetry Makes It Easier To Sound Grand

Shakespeare uses <u>poetry</u> to make what he's writing about <u>fancier</u>. Check it out:

This is the opening of *Richard III*. Richard is talking about how the civil wars are over and a new Yorkist King has brought peace.

RICHARD	Now is the winter of our discontent, Made glorious summer by this son of York, And all the clouds that loured upon our House In the deep bosom of the ocean buried. Now are our brows bound with victorious wreaths, Our bruised arms hung up for monuments, Our stern alarums changed to merry meetings, Our dreadful marches to delightful measures.

Going from bad to poor to verse...

I reckon it's ridiculous. But people didn't think it was ridiculous then. Shakespeare wrote in verse when a posh character was speaking, or when he wanted his writing to sound more <u>awesome</u>. And remember — Nine times out of ten when prose crops up it means someone common is talking.

The Language

It's easy to lose marks in your SAT because you feel <u>intimidated</u> by the <u>bizarre language</u> in Shakespeare. Don't be — the <u>weird stuff</u> is there for a <u>reason</u>, and it's nothing to be scared of.

Rhymed Verse Sounds Even Grander

Shakespeare's verse <u>doesn't always rhyme</u> — the important thing is that the words fit a <u>rhythm</u>.

But sometimes Shakespeare does use rhyme to create a <u>special effect</u>.
He uses rhyme to sound <u>even grander</u> than usual.

When shall we three meet again
In thunder, lightning, or in rain?
When the hurlyburly's done,
When the battle's lost and won.

Hubble-bubble...   ...toil and trouble...

...rhyming's grand
the fun's just double!

The witches in Macbeth speak in rhyme.
It makes 'em sound eerie and magical.

The Prince in Romeo And Juliet speaks in rhyme.
This makes him sound all serious and authoritative.

For never was a story of more woe
Than this of Juliet and her Romeo.

Don't Worry About The Funny Old Words

<u>Don't be put off</u> — it's normally pretty <u>obvious</u> what they mean.

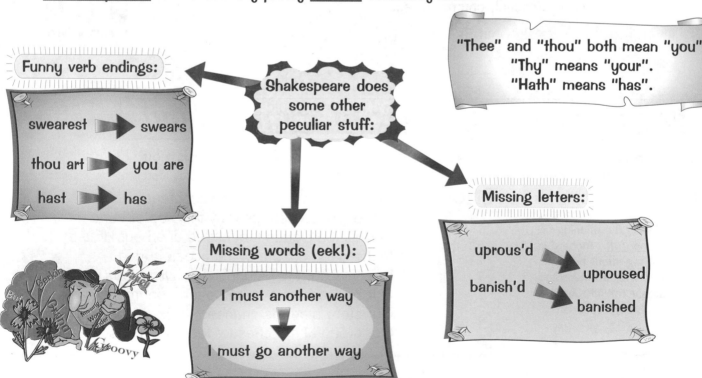

Funny verb endings:

swearest ➡ swears

thou art ➡ you are

hast ➡ has

Shakespeare does some other peculiar stuff:

"Thee" and "thou" both mean "you".
"Thy" means "your".
"Hath" means "has".

Missing letters:

uprous'd ➡ uproused

banish'd ➡ banished

Missing words (eek!):

I must another way
⬇
I must go another way

Do the opposite in song — inverse in verse...

When Shakespeare makes his verses rhyme, you can almost bet money it's to sound even <u>grander</u>. And don't turn your nose up at the strange old words — replace them in your mind with normal ones.

The Language

Think back to the writing section when I told you about ways of <u>comparing</u> things —
Shakespeare does this <u>loads</u>, and you'll get <u>great</u> marks for writing about how he does it.

You Have To Write About Comparisons

Shakespeare <u>loves</u> comparing things to other things.
Sometimes he'll give you a helping hand by making it really <u>obvious</u> that he's doing this.

> But mine is all as hungry as the sea
> And can digest as much:

The words "as ... as" show you Shakespeare is making a comparison. Here the Duke in *Twelfth Night* is comparing his love to the sea.

Sometimes it's a bit less obvious — and you've got to be <u>sharp</u> to notice he's doing it.

What light through yonder window breaks?

> ROMEO He jests at scars that never felt a wound.—
>   [JULIET *appears above at a window.*]
>   But soft! what light through yonder window breaks?
>   It is the east, and Juliet is the sun!

Romeo says that Juliet is like the sun, and when she appears at the window it's like the sun rising in the east.

In an exam, you would get marks for saying things like this — the sun gives brightness and warmth, so by comparing Juliet to the sun, Romeo is saying that Juliet lights up his life and makes him feel warm.

The Characters Seem To Speak In Riddles

Every morning a man gets a lift to the 12th floor of the building, gets out and walks the last 4 floors to his office on the 16th floor. Why?

This is really <u>annoying</u> at first. The characters don't mean exactly what they say. But you'll get great marks if you can <u>figure</u> it out and <u>explain</u> what they actually do mean.

> CHORUS Now old desire doth on his death-bed lie,
>   And young affection gapes to be his heir;
>   That fair for which love groan'd for, and would die,
>   With tender Juliet match'd, is not now fair.

The chorus is talking about the way that Romeo's love for Rosaline died when he saw Juliet and fell in love with her.

The chorus talks about Romeo's love for Rosaline — "old desire" — as if it is a person, "on his death-bed". And his love for Juliet — "young affection" — is compared to an heir, waiting to take the old love's place.

The King will never get my riddle.

> If you can look into the seeds of time,
> And say which grain will grow, and which will not

This is a quote from Banquo in Macbeth. He's talking about how difficult it is to predict what will happen in the future.

Never mind Romeo, my dog always p... oh, you said riddles...

You can get loads of marks in your SAT for talking about how Shakespeare uses comparisons.
If you can explain what it means when the characters are saying <u>weird</u> things, you'll be well away.

Other Strange Things

Some of the things the characters do seem really <u>strange</u> to us. Remember, though,
that it was all written <u>400 years</u> ago — and Shakespeare chose some very <u>odd</u> settings.

The Character Names Look Odd

Don't be put off by the fact that some of the characters have <u>funny</u> looking names.
Shakespeare set some of his plays in <u>foreign</u> countries and gave the characters foreign names.

Mercutio	Benvolio	Romeo

> On the head Romeo...
> Pronto-pronto Mercutio!
> Man-on Benvolio...

No, not the Italian footy team's midfield — they're characters from Romeo
And Juliet. They sound Italian because the play's set in Verona, in Italy.

> Burrp

Sir Toby Belch

Sometimes the character <u>names</u> are supposed to be <u>funny</u>.
Don't worry if you don't find them <u>side-splittingly hilarious</u>.
People's sense of <u>humour</u> in Shakespeare's day was <u>different</u>.

Life Was Different Back Then

Remember that things have <u>changed</u> a lot since Shakespeare's day — plus Shakespeare
set some of his plays even further back in the past — when things seem <u>even odder</u>.

In Romeo And Juliet there are
people fighting duels, and thirteen-
year-old girls being forced into
arranged marriages. This was all
common practice in those days.

> Don't forget — you're getting married tomorrow, Juliet. I've sorted it all out.
> Errrm, don't you think I'm a little young, Mum?

Macbeth is set in 11th century
Scotland. People believed in
witches a lot more than they do
nowadays, so the characters of
the witches would've seemed real.

The unearthing of the infamous
boxing amethyst of Barrow-in-Furness...

...world renowned in the
field of fighting jewels.

Henry V is about an English king who lived 600 years ago.
The country was ruled by dukes and earls, and bishops and
archbishops had greater power than they do now.

It's easy to get <u>put off</u> by how freaky some Shakespeare seems. Remember that the world
Shakespeare writes about is radically <u>different</u> from our world — then the plays will be <u>a doddle</u>.

People fighting jewels? — Oh, fighting DUELS...

OK, so you didn't need me to tell you that Shakespeare's odd. But remember that a lot of it's
just the way things were back then. Marriage at 13? They'd never allow it nowadays...

Revision Summary Questions

As if reading and writing tests weren't bad enough, you're stuck with doing Shakespeare as well. Shakespeare can be really intimidating — especially if you're not used to it. The language is old and funny looking and often it doesn't seem to make any sense at all. But read this section and have a go, and you'll be able to pick up bits of it. And then some more bits, and some more...
So make sure you've learned this section well enough to answer all these questions.

1) What is the three-point plan to Shakespeare SAT success?

2) You'll get good marks simply by showing you understand what's going on. True or false?

3) How important is it to use lots of quotes?

4) Only one of these statements is true. Which one?
    a) You have to understand every single word of Shakespeare to do well in your SAT.
    b) You don't have to understand it all — you only have to know roughly what's happening.
    c) Shakespeare's plays were written in the 1960s by a Surbiton chartered accountant.

5) What's an Act?

6) And a Scene?

7) What are the three kinds of plays that Shakespeare wrote?

8) Why do Shakespeare's characters sometimes talk to themselves?

9) What does [Aside] mean when you see it in a Shakespeare play?

10) What does "Exeunt" mean?

11) Why is it useful to read the stage directions?

12) What does a director do?

13) Why are Shakespeare's plays written in funny language?

14) What should you do when you see a sentence with the words in a strange order?

15) When you're reading Shakespeare, should you pause at the end of each line, or only when you come to punctuation?

16) If the characters use a lot of words, does that mean they're saying a complicated thing?

17) What does it mean if a character is talking in poetry?

18) And what does it mean if they talk in prose?

19) What is one of the reasons Shakespeare writes in verse?

20) And why might he write in rhyming verse?

21) What do "thee" and "thou" mean?

22) What about "thy"? And "hath"?

23) When Shakespeare compares something to something else, what should you do?
    a) Wonder why he has to make everything so darned complicated.
    b) Write about it in your SAT.

24) You'll get good marks for showing you understand what Shakespeare's riddles mean. True or false?

25) Why do some of Shakespeare's characters have odd-sounding names?

26) Why do some of the things that happen in Shakespeare's plays seem strange to us?

So, what's all the fuss about shaking spears for anyway?

What You Get in the Exam

To cure people who are scared of <u>spiders</u>, they show them lots of spiders. If you've got exam-phobia, look at this page — you'll know what to expect in the exam, and it won't <u>freak you out</u>.

You have to Write About your Set Scenes

You will study <u>one</u> Shakespeare <u>play</u> for your exam.

You will be told the <u>set scenes</u> for the play you're studying. The set scenes are <u>important</u> because your <u>exam question</u> will <u>focus</u> on them.

> You have to write about the set scenes <u>in detail</u> in the exam and show you know them <u>inside-out</u>.

You have to know about the <u>rest of the play</u> as well — but not in as much detail.

Here's How the Shakespeare Question Works

1) Bits from the scenes will be printed <u>on the exam paper</u>, and a good job too — you can remind yourself <u>what happens</u> and <u>get quotes</u> for your essay. They'll probably give you one <u>whole</u> scene and a <u>bit</u> from another one.

> Maybe I should add some Orcs to the Battle of Agincourt...

2) <u>Read</u> the scenes through <u>before</u> you try answering the question.

3) Keep <u>looking back</u> to them as you write your answer.

4) This is what the actual question will <u>look like</u>:

> <u>Stick to these bits</u> of the play in your answer. Write about <u>both</u> or you'll lose a ton of marks.

Henry V
Act 3 Scene 1
Act 4 Scene 7, lines 51 to 113

How does Shakespeare make the battles in Henry V seem exciting and important?
You should comment on:
• Henry's language
• what he says about the battles
• Montjoy's role in the play

Support your ideas with references to the following extracts.

> This is the actual question (obviously). Don't write about whatever comes into your head — <u>answer the question</u>.

> Sometimes questions will give you a list of <u>bullet points</u> like this. Use them to help <u>structure</u> your answer.

> This means "back up everything you say with quotes". <u>They mean it</u>. You'll get <u>twice as many</u> marks if you do.

Make quick notes — play a trumpet on Concorde...

OK, here we go. Once you've got <u>started</u>, it's not so scary. <u>Read</u> the questions and the bit of the play carefully, <u>use</u> the hints you're given, and above all, <u>don't panic</u>. Then you'll be fine.

Preparing Your Answer

There are two things you've got to do in the test <u>before</u> you put pen to paper — <u>work out what the question wants</u>, and <u>plan</u> your answer. Seems like a bit of a <u>hassle</u> but it's totally <u>worth it</u>.

Check Exactly What the Task is Asking For

It's a good idea to <u>start</u> by <u>reading through</u> the bits from the scenes. Now have a good look at exactly what the <u>question</u> is asking you to do.

These are the <u>most important words</u> in the question. This is what you'd have to <u>write about</u>.

> **What <u>different kinds of love</u> does Shakespeare introduce to the audience in these opening scenes?**
>
> Support your ideas with references to the following extracts.

1) Go through the scenes again, <u>underlining</u> words that look like they'll help <u>answer the question</u>.
2) For this one it would be a good start to underline the word '<u>love</u>' wherever it comes up.
3) Then go through <u>again</u> looking for any <u>less obvious</u> bits about love.

> ORSINO   If <u>music</u> be the food of love, play on —
> Give me excess of it, that, surfeiting,
> The appetite may sicken, and so die.

You get about <u>45 minutes</u> for this question — spend at least <u>10 minutes</u> reading and planning.

Plan Your Essay

Before you start writing <u>MAKE A PLAN</u>.

1)	It'll help you <u>get your ideas straight</u>.
2)	You can arrange your points in a <u>sensible order</u>.
3)	It should mean you <u>don't forget</u> anything important.

This essay's about <u>different kinds of love</u>. So <u>write down</u> all the different kinds of love you've spotted in the scenes.

Write down any <u>comments</u> you've got about each one.

Scribble down where you can get <u>good quotes</u> to back up each point.

Decide on the best <u>order</u> to write about your points.

1. <u>ROMANTIC LOVE</u>
Act 1, Scene 1 — Orsino <u>says</u> in love with Olivia — but talks about <u>his</u> feelings, not much about <u>her</u>. A bit fake? In love with being in love?

3. 2. <u>FRIENDSHIP</u>
Act 1, Scene 2 — V and Captain friends

4. 3. <u>FAMILY LOVE AND CONCERN</u>
Act 1, Scene 2 — V loves brother — worried about him.

2. 4. <u>FLIPPANT ATTITUDE TO LOVE</u>
Act 1, Scene 3 — Sir T teases Olivia about loving Sir A — doesn't take love seriously

5. <u>OPPOSITE OF LOVE — GRIEF</u>
Act 1, Scenes 1, 2 and 3 — O's brother recently died. Not interested in romantic love — at the moment.

If music be the food of love — play me a pizza...

It really is <u>ultra-important</u> to make sure you know what you're supposed to write about before you start. If you don't do what the task says, you won't get the <u>marks</u>. That's the simple truth.

Why Characters Do Things

You can't predict exactly what they'll ask you in the exam — but some types of questions do come up a lot. Questions <u>about the characters</u> and why they do things are pretty common.

Write about What They're Like

> **Much Ado About Nothing**
> Act 1 Scene 3 and Act 2 Scene 2
>
> **What kind of character is Don John and why does he try to spoil Claudio and Hero's marriage?**
>
> Support your ideas by referring to the scenes.

For this question you need to go through the scene to find the bits that tell you <u>what Don John is like</u> and <u>what he thinks of Claudio and Hero</u>.

It helps if you go into the test with a pretty good idea about what the characters are like and what they do in the <u>rest</u> of the play.

Go through the Scenes and Make Notes

> *Don John is pretty nasty. He calls himself a "plain-dealing villain."*
>
> *Don John has been beaten in a war by Don Pedro. That's why he hates Claudio — Don Pedro's "right hand" man.*
>
> *He's in a bad mood in Act 1, Scene 3 and says that ruining Claudio's marriage will make him feel better.*
>
> *He encourages Borachio to carry out a plan to ruin the marriage — "any impediment will be medicinable to me."*

Note down quotes. You'll need them later.

Watch when Characters talk About Each Other

Characters talk about each other — this gives you <u>useful information</u> about them. E.g. Here's what Beatrice and Hero say about <u>Don John</u> in Act 2 Scene 1.

| BEATRICE | How tartly that gentleman looks! I never can see him but I am heart-burned an hour after. |
| HERO | He is of a very melancholy disposition. |

You can find out a lot about the person <u>making</u> the comment as well as the person they're talking about. E.g. Don John sounds pretty <u>bitter</u> when he talks about Claudio.

DON JOHN That young start-up hath all the glory of my overthrow.

Why Characters Do Things

Remember, you're <u>only</u> expected to write about the <u>bits</u> of the play that they've <u>given you</u> to read. You <u>can</u> find an answer in there, if you look.

Get as Much as You Can from the Set Scenes

If you look at the scenes <u>thoroughly</u>, you can work out a lot about the characters.

Don John doesn't mind being thought of as a bad man. He says in Act 1 Scene 3 that he doesn't see the point of pretending to be nice to people just to make them happy. He even describes himself as a "plain-dealing villain."

Remember who's Who

When writing about a character remember to talk about what their <u>position is in society</u> and <u>how they're related</u> to the other characters.

Remember to <u>quote</u> to show where your answer comes from.

Who? Oooh.. YES that's right. I am Don Juan.

Don John is illegitimate, so he will never have the wealth and social status which his half-brother Don Pedro has. This is part of the reason why Don John is so bitter and resentful. He is constantly looking for ways to dishonour and humiliate Don Pedro and his friends. He says "to despite them I will endeavour anything."

In Shakespeare's time there was a lot of stigma associated with being born outside of marriage. Shakespeare's audience would have expected a character who was illegitimate to be a troublemaker. Don John is therefore a bit of a stereotypical villain.

Write about the Way that Characters Speak

Shakespeare gives the audience a <u>picture</u> of the characters by what they <u>say</u> and <u>how</u> they say it, <u>just</u> as much as by what they <u>do</u>.

Don John talks in prose in these scenes. Shakespeare generally used poetry for the more romantic and distinguished characters and prose for the more ordinary characters. Characters like Claudio and Don Pedro speak a lot in poetry because they're the heroes of the play. The prose spoken by Don John contrasts with this — it emphasises his outsider status from the other nobles.

Plays are full of vehicles pretending — 'car actors'...

<u>Read</u> the scenes carefully to find all the bits that tell you what the characters are <u>like</u>. Pay extra special attention to things they <u>say</u> about each other, and <u>how</u> they speak. Remember <u>who</u> the characters are — what their <u>relationships</u> are, and if they're the <u>king</u> or the <u>village idiot</u> or whatever.

How Characters Persuade

You might get a question about <u>how characters persuade</u> — especially for a play like <u>Henry V</u> where's there's a shedload of big speeches.

Here's a Classic Persuading Question

Henry V
Act 3 Scene 1
Act 3 Scene 2, lines 1-56

How effective is the speech that King Henry uses to motivate his troops?

Support your ideas with references to the following extracts.

1) To make your answer <u>really good</u> you'll have to make several points in your answer.

2) The <u>main things</u> you can write about for this question are the <u>language</u> Henry uses, and what effect it has on all the <u>other characters</u> who appear in these two scenes.

① Write about the Tricks of Persuasive Language

This is where you get to write about all the <u>tricks</u> of Shakespeare's <u>language</u> — see Section 4.

Look at the words he uses.

> In peace, there's nothing so becomes a man,
> as modest stillness and humility:
> But when the blast of war blows in our ears,
> then imitate the action of the tiger:

The king <u>compares</u> the way a man should behave in <u>war</u> to the way he should behave in <u>peacetime</u>.

> then lend the eye a terrible aspect:
> Let it pry through the portage of the head,
> Like the brass cannon;

He compares the eyes to a <u>cannon</u> — a good <u>warlike</u> simile.

He's saying that the English are descended from men like <u>Alexander the Great</u> to make them feel <u>proud</u> and <u>brave</u>.

> On, on, you noblest English,
> Whose blood is fet from fathers of war-proof:
> Fathers, that like so many Alexanders,
> Have in these parts from morn till even fought.

The king is saying that the troops would be <u>shaming their parents</u> by <u>giving up</u> the fight.

> Dishonour not your mothers: now attest
> That those whom you called fathers did beget you!

Gosh, what a persuasive speech — off I go to war!

> I see you stand like greyhounds in the slips,
> Straining upon the start. The game's afoot:
> Follow your spirit; and upon this charge,
> Cry 'God for Harry, England, and Saint George'

He deliberately <u>assumes</u> they'll all be raring to go.

Here's a nice bit of <u>patriotic shouting</u> to end with.

How Characters Persuade

② Write about What the Soldiers do

When you plan your answer, look at the first 28 lines of scene 2 and jot down what the soldiers are doing.

Bardolph wants to fight — Nym doesn't want to — he's afraid of being hurt (quote "the knocks are too hot..."). The boy would rather be in the pub, and so would Pistol. The soldiers don't want to fight, so they haven't been persuaded by the King's speech.

Well I'm <u>not</u> persuaded, I'm SCARED!

Nym

③ Write about what the Boy says

This is part of an answer that talks about what the Boy says.

Each time the answer makes a <u>point</u>, there's a <u>quote</u>.

The Boy says he knows what the three soldiers are like. He thinks they're not real men: "Though they would serve me, could not be man to me, for indeed three such antics do not amount to a man"

Bardolph acts brave but isn't. He "faces it out, but fights not". Pistol "breaks words and keeps whole weapons," which means that he has a sharp tongue but doesn't use his sword. Nym, on the other hand, doesn't say much. We can see that he doesn't do much in battle either: "his few bad words are matched with as few good deeds, for 'a never broke any man's head but his own, and that was against a post, when he was drunk."

This bit answers the question. The King's speech <u>wasn't</u> very effective.

The boy's speech shows us that Bardolph, Pistol and Nym are lazy, drunken, cowardly thieves — the boy tells us stories of how they stole a lute-case and a shovel. They haven't changed at all since they listened to the King's speech, which shows that the speech wasn't very effective.

You could also say the soldiers are truly bad men, so nothing that the King could say would ever make them brave.

A wallet on the scales — Purse-weighed...

This is **NOT THAT BAD**... there are <u>two things</u> you have to write about for persuasion questions — the <u>words</u> the character uses, and what the other characters <u>say and do</u> in reaction to their words.

Imagine You're Directing a Scene

These are 10 out of 10 for <u>fun</u>.*

*on a scale where 1 is having 10 teeth pulled, and 10 is having one tooth pulled

Think about the Audience

Directing a play means deciding <u>how</u> you want to <u>show</u> the <u>story</u> to the <u>audience</u>.

The <u>actors</u> have to play their parts so that the <u>audience</u> understand what's happening — and <u>feel</u> all the different <u>moods</u> that Shakespeare wanted them to feel when he wrote the play. That's what <u>you</u> have to <u>write about</u> in your <u>answer</u>.

The Audience Don't Have the Script in front of them

<u>You</u> have to <u>make</u> the audience understand what's happening — here are several ways to do this.

ANGRY SHOUTING

I'm ANGRY!

SHUT UP!

Ms. Angry

Make the actors <u>say</u> their lines in a way that <u>shows</u> the <u>feelings</u> of the character.

Hee hee, I'm so evil!

EVIL CLOTHES

Mr. Evil

Show the audience what a character is <u>like</u> by the <u>clothes</u> they wear.

Show the audience the <u>mood</u> of a scene by <u>lighting</u> and <u>sound</u>.

BLUE MOONLIGHT

SWEET MUSIC

I feel all romantic.

Mr. Romantic

You can write about all these things in your <u>answer</u>.

You have to Understand the Scene

Once again, <u>you</u> have to understand what's going on, because <u>you</u> have to say how you would <u>show</u> the <u>audience</u> what's going on.

That means you need to understand the <u>language</u>.

| 1ST WITCH | Pour in sow's blood, that hath eaten
Her nine farrow; grease that's sweaten
From the murderer's gibbet throw
Into the flame |

TERRIBLE THINGS

SUGAR

Sweetened grease?

NO!

The witch is talking about <u>terrible</u> things — a pig who's eaten her piglets and the sweat of a hanged man.

If you <u>don't understand</u> what a character's on about, it's very difficult to tell if they're sad, happy or angry.

Imagine You're Directing a Scene

Write about the Mood of the Scene

The <u>mood</u> of the scene is really important for this type of question.
Some scenes are <u>funny</u>, some are <u>scary</u>, some are full of <u>excitement</u>
and <u>tension</u>, some are <u>spooky</u> and some are <u>romantic</u>.

The mood of this scene is
<u>frightening</u> and <u>supernatural</u>.

Thrice and once the
hedge-pig whined.

NO! It should be scary!

THE <u>WRONG</u>
MOOD

1ST WITCH	Thrice the brinded cat hath mewed.
2ND WITCH	Thrice and once the hedge-pig whined.
3RD WITCH	Harpier cries: — 'Tis time, 'tis time
1ST WITCH	Round about the cauldron go:
	In the poisoned entrails throw.
	Toad that under cold stone
	Days and nights has thirty-one
	Sweltered venom sleeping got,
	Boil thou first i'th charméd pot

The mood of the scene you get will be pretty clear. What you have to do in
your answer is say <u>which bits</u> show the mood of the scene more than others.

You've Guessed it — Quote Lots

If you want an actor to <u>speak</u> a line in a <u>particular way</u>, then <u>write</u> that down. Give a quote.

I'll need all of these
for loads of quotes.

*Macbeth should say his lines as if he is trying very
hard to pretend he isn't frightened. When he says
"Had I three ears, I'd hear thee" he should laugh a
little, as if he is trying to joke with the apparition.*

Quote a bit of the scene that really shows
you what the <u>mood</u> of the scene is.

Mood — the sound cows made...

The trick to writing about <u>directing</u> a scene is to think about the <u>audience's point of view</u>. You have
to <u>show</u> them what the <u>mood</u> of the scene is — with <u>lights</u>, <u>sound</u>, and the <u>way</u> things are <u>said</u>.

Imagining You Are a Character

These "Imagine you are..." questions are a lot <u>harder</u> than they look.
<u>Don't</u> go thinking you've got an easy ride if this is what they give you in the test.

Questions Like this are Very Hard

You have to <u>pretend</u> to be one of the <u>characters</u> from the play for these questions.
Writing as if you're <u>someone else</u> is <u>tons harder</u> than answering the question as <u>yourself</u>.

> In these scenes Juliet thinks about her situation and decides to take the potion the Friar has given her.
>
> **Imagine you are Juliet. Write your thoughts and feelings explaining why you have chosen to take this desperate action.**

You've got to do <u>four things</u> for this question:

1) Write from <u>Juliet's point of view</u>.
2) Say what she <u>thinks</u>.
3) Say how she <u>feels</u>.
4) Explain exactly <u>why</u> she's going through with the Friar's plan.

It's really important that you do <u>everything</u> the question asks.

This is What You Get Marks For

<u>Picking out</u> bits of the scene that answer the question.

<u>Quoting</u> to back up what you say.

Writing as a character makes it a lot <u>harder</u> to quote.

Saying what <u>you think</u> about the bits of the scene you've picked out.

That's the <u>same stuff</u> you get marks for in any type of question.
Your answers for character questions have got to be just as <u>detailed</u>.

Clever Answers Don't always Pick up the Marks

You <u>are</u> supposed to write as Juliet, don't forget. The <u>problem</u> comes if you do that
<u>utterly brilliantly</u> and <u>forget</u> to do the other things. Go through the scene bit by bit,
write about the <u>events</u> and stick in some <u>quotes</u> — that's what'll get you the marks.

Don't get blown away — just remember to put in
all the bits that you know make a good answer.

I know, I know, it doesn't seem fair,
but that's the way it is...

Imagining You Are A Character

You Have to be Ace at Writing About Emotions

Be sure that you can write a good long answer about Juliet's emotions for this question.

I'm really upset because I might not see Romeo again.

You're going to have to come up with a whole lot more than that.

What a total bummer...

There's more to it than writing about what happens in the scenes. You have to think about how it makes Juliet feel.

Look at the words she uses and see if they give an idea of her emotions.
Think about what she's like and what's happened to her in the rest of the play, too.

Yes, you Have to Quote

Quoting is very difficult in these questions, but you still have to do it.

I cannot consent to marry again. I am already married to Romeo, and I cannot break God's law. "God joined my heart to Romeo, thee our hands".

Juliet's hardly likely to put long quotes in her own thoughts. She might think about something that someone's said to her.

A short quote looks natural.

I shuddered when Paris said to me: "Thy face is mine". No part of me is his. I am Romeo's, and I would rather die than betray him.

Don't think you can get away without putting quotes in though.

Imagine — and other John Lennon classics...

The funny thing with the Shakespeare paper is that sometimes hard questions are disguised as easy ones, and easy questions are disguised as hard ones. These "imagine you are" questions are definitely of the difficult variety. Hard cheese if you get one, I'm afraid.

Writing Your Answer

All the questions are different, but there are a few <u>basic points</u> that'll help you do any of them.

Watch your Paragraphs, Sentences and Spelling

It's no good understanding the play if you don't <u>write well</u>.
Here are some tips on impressing the examiner with what you write.

1) Think about what you want to say, and make sure your <u>sentences</u> are good and clear.

2) Every time you make a new point, start a new <u>paragraph</u>.

3) Link your points <u>together</u> well.

Use phrases like "Another way that Shakespeare creates tension is..."

4) Take care with those <u>spellings</u>.

And watch your step, too.

Don't forget to Quote

Quoting is the key. If you <u>don't quote</u>, you <u>won't get the marks</u> — it really <u>is</u> that simple.

It all hinges on this...

Remember, the whole purpose of quoting is to <u>back up</u> a <u>point</u> you've made.

Here's an example...

> Apart from Romeo, neither side wants to avoid a fight. As soon as Tybalt speaks, Mercutio is keen to bring up the idea of fighting.
> "And but one word with one of us? Couple it with something, make it a word and a blow."

If you're quoting more than one line, put the quote in a separate paragraph.

Arrgghhh...

oOOffff

If I have to stop this car one more time...

ROMEO

Make a <u>point</u>, give a <u>quote</u> and <u>explain why</u> you've used the quote.

Cheap plumbers — they give the best quotes...

In <u>every single paragraph</u>, aim to <u>QUOTE</u>. You'd have to be some sort of <u>nutter</u> to forget to quote after reading this page. If you quote well in your <u>SAT</u>, you're onto a <u>winner</u>.

Huge Revision Question

Here's a lovely exam type question on *Twelfth Night*, all about extracts from Act 3 Scene 4 and Act 4 Scene 1. It's the length of extract and the kind of question you'll get in the exam. Write out a good answer — make sure you practise all the tricks from this section.

> In these scenes, the characters are confused between Viola and Sebastian.
>
> **Describe how Shakespeare shows this confusion to the audience.**

Support your ideas with references to the following extracts.

ACT 3 SCENE 4 lines 300-394
Before Olivia's house

SIR TOBY	[*to Viola*] There's no remedy, sir, he will fight with you for oath's sake: marry, he hath better bethought him of his quarrel, and he finds that now scarce to be worth talking of; therefore draw for the supportance of his vow, he protests he will not hurt you.	300
VIOLA	[*aside*] Pray God defend me! A little thing would make me tell them how much I lack of a man.	
FABIAN	Give ground, if you see him furious.	
SIR TOBY	Come, Sir Andrew, there's no remedy, the gentleman will for his honour's sake have one hour with you: he cannot by the duello avoid it: but he has promised me, as he is a gentleman and a soldier, he will not hurt you. Come on, to't!	305
SIR ANDREW	Pray God, he keep his oath!	
VIOLA	I do assure you, 'tis against my will.	

They make ready to fight; Antonio enters

ANTONIO	[*to Sir Andrew*] Put up your sword:if this young gentleman Have done offence, I take the fault on me; If you offend him, I defy you.	310
SIR TOBY	You, sir! why, what are you?	
ANTONIO	One, sir, that for his love dares yet do more Than you have heard him brag to you he will.	315
SIR TOBY	Nay, if you are an undertaker, I am for you.	

They draw
Two officers approach

FABIAN	O good Sir Toby, hold; here come the officers	
SIR TOBY	[*to Antonio*] I'll be with you anon.	

He hides from the officers behind a tree

VIOLA	Pray, sir, put your sword up, if you please.	
SIR ANDREW	Marry, I will, sir, and for that I promised you, I'll be good as any word. He will bear you easily and reins well	320
1ST OFFICER	This is the man, do thy office	
2ND OFFICER	Antonio, I do arrest thee at the suit Of count Orsino.	
ANTONIO	You do mistake me sir.	325
1ST OFFICER	No, slr, no jot; I know your favour well: Though now you have no sea-cap on your head... Take him away, he knows I know him well.	
ANTONIO	I must obey. [*to Viola*] This comes with seeking you; But there's no remedy, I shall answer it... What will you do, now my necessity Makes me to ask for my purse? It grieves me	330

Huge Revision Question

	Much more for what I cannot do for you	
	Than what befalls myself... You stand amazed,	
	But be of comfort.	335
2ND OFFICER	Come, sir, away.	
ANTONIO	I must entreat of you some of that money.	
VIOLA	What money, sir?	
	For the fair kindness you have showed me here,	
	And part being prompted by your present trouble,	340
	Out of my lean and low ability	
	I'll lend you something... My having is not much,	
	I'll make division of my present with you:	
	Hold, here's half my coffer.	
ANTONIO	Will you deny me now?	345
	Is't possible that my deserts to you	
	Can lack persuasion? Do not tempt my misery,	
	Lest that it make me so unsound a man	
	As to upbraid you with those kindnesses	
	That I have done for you.	350
VIOLA	I know of none	
	Nor know I you by voice or any feature:	
	I hate ingratitude more in a man,	
	Than lying vainness, babbling drunkenness	
	Or any taint of vice whose strong corruption	355
	Inhabits our frail blood.	
ANTONIO	O heavens themselves!	
2ND OFFICER	Come, sir, I pray you go.	
ANTONIO	Let me speak a little.	
	The youth that you see here	360
	I snatched one half out of the jaws of death	
	Relieved him with such sanctity of love,	
	And to his image, which methought did promise	
	Most venerable worth, did I devotion	
1ST OFFICER	What's that to us? the time goes by: away!	365
ANTONIO	But, O, how vile an idol proves this god!	
	Thou hast, Sebastian, done good feature shame.	
	In nature there's no blemish but the mind;	
	None can be called deformed but the unkind:	
	Virtue us beauty, but the beauteous evil	370
	Are empty trunks o'erflourished by the devil.	
2ND OFFICER	The man grows mad, away with him!	
	Come, come, sir.	
ANTONIO	Lead me on.	
	They carry him off	
VIOLA	Methinks his words do from such passion fly,	375
	That he believes himself — so do not I?	
	Prove true, o imagination, O prove true,	
	That I, dear brother, be now ta'en for you!	
SIR TOBY	Come hither, knight, come hither, Fabian; we'll whisper o'er a couplet	
	or two of most sage saws.	380
VIOLA	He named Sebastian; I my brother know	
	Yet living in my glass; even such and so	
	In favour was my brother, and he went	
	Still in this fashion, colour, ornament,	

Huge Revision Question

	For him I imitate: O if it prove,	385
	Tempests are kind and salt waves fresh in love!	
	She goes	
SIR TOBY	A very dishonest paltry boy, and more a coward than a hare. His dishonesty appears in	
	leaving his friend here in necessity and denying him; and for his cowardship, ask Fabian.	
FABIAN	A coward, a most devout coward, religious in it.	
SIR ANDREW	'Slid, I'll after him again and beat him.	390
SIR TOBY	Do, cuff him soundly, but never draw thy sword.	
SIR ANDREW	An I do not, —	
FABIAN	Come, let's see the event	
SIR TOBY	I dare lay any money, 'twill be nothing yet.	
	Thoy follow	

ACT 4 SCENE 1, line 1-line 32
Before Olivia's house

FESTE	Will you make me believe that I am not sent for you?	
SEBASTIAN	Go to, go to, thou art a foolish fellow; Let me be clear of thee.	
FESTE	Well hold out, i' faith! No, I do not know you, nor am I sent to you by my lady	
	to bid you come speak with her, nor your name is not Master Cesario,	
	nor this is not my nose neither: nothing that is so, is so.	5
SEBASTIAN	I prithee, vent thy folly somewhere else,	
	Thou knowst not me.	
FESTE	Vent my folly! He has heard that word of some great man and now applies it to a fool.	
	Vent my folly! I am afraid this great lubber, the world will prove a cockney...	
	I prithee now, ungird thy strangeness and tell me what I shall vent to my lady:	10
	shall I vent to her that thou art coming?	
SEBASTIAN	I prithee, foolish Greek, depart from me.	
	There's money for thee: if you tarry longer	
	I shall give worse payment.	
FESTE	By my troth, thou hast an open hand... These wise men that give fools money get	15
	themselves a good report — after fourteen years' purchase.	
	Sir Andrew enters, Sir Toby and Fabian following	
SIR ANDREW	Now sir, have I met you again? there's for you. *[He strikes wide]*	
SEBASTIAN	*[Replies with his fists]* Why, there's for thee, and there, and there! *[He knocks him down]*	
SIR TOBY	*[Seizes him fom behind]* Hold, sir, or I'll throw your dagger o'er the house.	
FESTE	This I will tell my lady straight: I would not be in some of your coats for two pence.	20
	He goes	
SIR TOBY	Come on, sir! hold!	
SIR ANDREW	Nay, let him alone, I'll go another way to work with him: I'll have an action	
	of battery struck against him, if there be any law in Illyria: though I struck him first,	
	yet it's no matter for that.	
SEBASTIAN	Let go thy hand!	25
SIR TOBY	Come sir, I will not let you go. Come, my young soldier, put up your iron:	
	you are well fleshed... Come on.	
SEBASTIAN	I will be free from thee...*[He throws him off]* What would'st thou now? *[He draws]*	
	If thou dar'st tempt me further, draw thy sword.	
SIR TOBY	What, what? *[He also draws]* Nay then, I must have an ounce or two of this	30
	malapert blood from thee.	

What You Have to Do

Writing... a <u>tough nut</u> to crack. Unless you're a squirrel that is.

You Have to do Two Writing Questions

There are <u>two</u> parts to the Writing Paper:

1) <u>The Shakespeare Writing Question</u>: you have to write on a theme linked with the Shakespeare play you're studying.

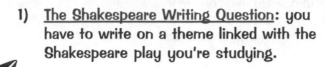

2) <u>The Long Writing Question</u>: you have to read a short bit of writing which sets the scene, then write something connected with that bit of writing.

Read the question all the way <u>through</u>...

IN THE SAT: Don't <u>rush</u> into doing the writing. Read the <u>questions</u> carefully before you start.

Show Off these Five things in Your Writing

The <u>examiners</u> want to see how good you are at the <u>nuts and bolts of writing</u>. Here's what they're looking for:

One... two... three... er... six?

1) <u>GOOD SPELLING</u>
So always <u>check</u> over what you've written for mistakes.

2) <u>PROPER SENTENCES</u>
i.e. sentences with <u>full punctuation</u>, that <u>make sense</u>.

3) <u>WELL-ORGANISED WRITING</u>
That means writing in <u>paragraphs</u>, having an <u>introduction</u> and a clear <u>ending</u>, and a sensible <u>order</u> to all the points you make in between.

4) <u>THE RIGHT STYLE</u>
e.g. If you're asked for a magazine article use <u>words</u> and <u>phrases</u> that make your writing <u>sound like</u> a magazine article.

5) <u>SIGNS YOU'VE THOUGHT ABOUT THE READER</u>
If it's a piece for <u>young kids</u> keep it <u>simple</u> so they can understand. If it's for your <u>gran</u> don't put in any <u>swearing</u>. Make sure it's <u>interesting</u> enough to keep your reader from nodding off too.

Insect writing exams — ants-er the question...

<u>Don't panic</u> when you're doing writing questions. Take a deep breath, read through the whole thing <u>carefully</u>, and remember what they're looking for — good writing not amazing ideas.

The Long Writing Question

The two writing questions aren't <u>wildly</u> different. But they're not exactly the same either — <u>learn the difference</u> now so you don't make any unfortunate boobs on the day.

The Long Writing Question Looks Like This...

There's quite <u>a lot</u> to read for these tasks. Read through it all <u>carefully</u> a couple of times, so you know <u>exactly</u> what it is they want you to do.

This bit of writing sets the scene. Read it <u>carefully</u>.

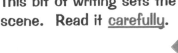

This is an extract from the paper the *Daily Hail*.

> ### *The Daily Hail*
>
> ## Fur Will Fly at No.10
>
> *The Editor writes:*
> What's going on at 10 Downing Street? First we learn that Humphrey the cat's not allowed in the offices. Now we learn he's been confined to the kitchen. And there's <u>no cat flap</u>. What kind of life is this for a cat that's served the nation for nine and a half years? I'm disgusted, Prime Minister, and I believe the British public is disgusted too.

As a reader of the "Daily Hail", write a letter to the Prime Minister, agreeing or disagreeing with the article.

This is what you've actually got to <u>do</u>.

1) <u>Pretend</u> you're someone who reads the "Daily Hail".
2) <u>Write a letter</u> to the <u>Prime Minister</u>. Use the right <u>language</u>, and <u>lay it out</u> like a proper letter.
3) <u>Agree</u> with the article... OR... <u>disagree</u> with the article.

What You Need to Know

1) You should spend <u>45 minutes</u> in total on this question. Spend <u>15 minutes</u> <u>planning</u>. Spend <u>25 minutes writing</u>. Leave about <u>5 minutes</u> at the end to check over what you've written.
2) It's called the 'long' writing question, but you <u>don't</u> have to write pages and pages. A bit over <u>300 words</u> should do it.

Don't get carried away

Deciding What to Say

You'll be able to use <u>ideas from the article</u> to work out what you're going to say.

For this question you could pick out all the points the editor makes, then agree or disagree with each point.

The Shakespeare Question

Did I hear a sigh of _boredom_ as you turned to this page... Just a little one... I'm sure I did...
These may not be the most interesting pages in the book, but they sure as ham are _useful_.

The Shakespeare Question Looks Like This...

It starts by linking the task to the _play_ you've studied.

Then there's a bit _setting the scene_ for the piece you've got to write.

You get a few points to write about. If it says _you should_ they mean it. Write about each bullet point in turn.

> In _Macbeth_, the ambitions of Macbeth and Lady Macbeth put them under huge pressure and stress.
>
> _The following is printed in your school newspaper:_
>
> Some people think too much pressure is put on young people to be high achievers. We want to know what _you_ think.
>
> You should write about:
> * the ways young people are expected to be successful, e.g. school, sports, appearance
> * who expects young people to be high achievers
> * what effects this pressure could have
>
> **Write the article for the school newspaper.**

If they say article they mean _article_. Don't go writing a letter or a speech.

What You Need to Know

1) You get _20 marks_ for this task.
2) Spend _10 minutes planning_ and _20_ writing.
3) This task's linked to the Shakespeare play you've studied, but you don't have to say _anything_ about the play. Stick to _answering the question_.
4) You need to write about _200 words_ for this one. Keep your writing _organised_ and _stick to the point_. You haven't got _time_ to write a long waffly essay.

Skip the waffle. Get straight to the point.

Always Use the Bullet Points

* Time's _short_.
* They give marks for _how well you write_, not for brilliant ideas.
* Using the bullet points is the _quickest_ way to get started.
* Don't pick and choose. Use _all of them_.

A Shakespeare task — wave your javelin about...

The two writing questions are a bit different, so you have to tackle them in different ways.
Not that different though. Not as different as a _cockroach_ and the Mona Lisa.

Work Out What To Say

Once you've read the question, work out <u>what</u> you're going to say to answer it.
That means making a <u>plan</u>.

Decide What To Say Before You Start

You've got to have a <u>good think</u> about what you're going to write about <u>before</u> you start.
You don't need to know exactly what you're going to write, but you need to have a rough idea.

> **Good writing <u>makes a point</u>. It doesn't just ramble on about nothing.**

Whether you're writing a story, a description, a letter or an opinion piece, make sure you've
got <u>enough ideas</u> to keep you writing till your time's up — without having to waffle.

Jot Down your Points into a Rough Plan

It's a good idea to jot down a <u>plan</u> of the points you want to make <u>before</u> you start writing.
That way you don't get to the end and realise you've <u>forgotten</u> something.

> Q. Write an article for a newspaper about an issue that's important to you.
> Explain why you think the issue is important.

① A plan doesn't have to be in proper sentences. It's just a <u>reminder</u> for you to use.

② <u>Start</u> with what you think is the <u>most important</u> point. This grabs your reader's attention.

③ Try to <u>link</u> your points together. You can link smoothly from meat to treatment of animals.

> PLAN: *Modern farming methods.*
>
> *Reducing quality of soil — less food can be grown — soon we won't have enough to eat.*
>
> *Risks to human health — pesticides — antibiotics in meat.*
>
> *Animals treated badly — profits more important than welfare.*
>
> *What we can do — buy organic.*

④ Work out how you're going to <u>end</u> your piece. This is a positive ending — it says what we can do.

<u>No rambling — so no walking boots needed...</u>

Obviously, writing that <u>rambles on</u> without getting anywhere <u>isn't</u> going to get the best <u>marks</u>.
Work out roughly what you're going to say <u>before</u> you start writing. It helps to jot down a <u>plan</u>.
All this needs to be second nature by the time you get to the Exam, so <u>get learning</u>.

Stories Need Planning Too

It's not only questions which ask for your opinion that need <u>planning</u>. You should <u>also</u> make a plan if you're doing a <u>story</u> question. Even <u>description</u> pieces will be better with a plan.

Plan What Will Happen In Your Story

It's tempting just to start by writing "once upon a time..." and hope that you'll be able to make up what happens in your story <u>as you go along</u>. But that's a <u>really bad</u> idea.

<u>Before</u> you start to write your story, you should have a good idea of how it's going to <u>end</u>, and what's going to happen in the <u>middle</u>. Otherwise you'll get in all sorts of <u>problems</u>.

Q. Write about an exciting journey you have made.
It can be real or imaginary.

PLAN: *Going on holiday on a plane.*

Everyone except me got very ill from the food.

Went to the cockpit — pilot was unconscious.

I talked to air traffic control over the pilot's radio and they told me what to do.

I landed the plane safely.

Everyone went to hospital — they were all fine.

This plan is like a <u>summary</u> of the story you're going to write.

When you write the <u>story</u>, you could have two or three paragraphs about <u>each</u> of these points.

You've <u>planned</u> how it's going to <u>end</u>, so you always know what you're aiming towards.

Even Description Pieces Need A Plan

When you're <u>describing</u> something, there isn't a beginning, a middle and an end like in a story. But you <u>still</u> need to know what kind of things you're going to say.

Quiet? Eh?

Q. Describe your favourite place.

PLAN: *Down by the river — peaceful and pretty — lots of grass — friends — go swimming in summer — ice skating in winter — friendly horse in nearby field — lots of trees — lovely colours in autumn — wild flowers in spring.*

It might not look like much, but notes like this can <u>really help</u> you. You're not going to get <u>stuck</u> and <u>panic</u> because you run out of ideas for things to write.

Stories need a quiche? — I said plan, not FLAN...

Whatever it is you've got to write, having a <u>plan</u> can really help you. If you start writing <u>without</u> a plan, you're likely to <u>run out</u> of ideas or find you're waffling on about nothing at all.

SECTION SIX — WRITING QUESTIONS

Use The Right Style

Using the right writing <u>style</u> to write your answer is very important. You'll <u>lose</u> marks if you choose the <u>wrong</u> style, or if you <u>change</u> styles halfway through your answer.

Write in the Right Style to Fit the Question

Each question needs you to write in a certain <u>style</u>. Look at what the question is <u>telling</u> you to do, and use your common sense to decide what style to write in.

If you're asked to write a travel brochure, use loads of <u>fancy phrases</u> — like this.

Golden sandy beaches and gently lapping waves await you on the island of Noonos. Soak up the sun and forget your worldly cares with a refreshing swim in the warm, crystal-clear sea...

The faulty pelican crossing has caused ten accidents. Do you want to run that risk? We must take action now before someone else is injured — or even killed. Write to your local councillor at once.

If the question tells you to write a speech, be <u>snappy</u>, <u>punchy</u> and <u>direct</u> — like this.

If the question tells you to write a <u>horror</u> story, use words that give a feeling of <u>fear</u> and <u>suspense</u> — like this.

Slowly, the thick oak door creaked open. Emma quaked with fear. The clock ticked loudly. Then — bang! The ear-piercing crack of a gunshot filled the room. Emma screamed.

Use Fancy Words if you Need them

Some writing styles tend to involve lots of fancy words.
Don't be afraid to use them — but only if you're <u>sure</u> you know what they <u>mean</u>.

The important thing is to show you <u>know</u> what kind of style you're supposed to be using.
You'll get marks for <u>trying</u> — even if the spelling of the long words is a bit wonky.

Like a Makeover show — it's a Style Challenge...

It's very important that you get the <u>style</u> right — or at least that you <u>show</u> you <u>understand</u> what sort of style you should be using. Make sure that's in your mind when you answer the question.

Writing Letters

It's especially important to get your writing style right when you have to write a <u>letter</u>.
If you're asked to write a letter, sort out whether it's <u>formal</u> or <u>informal</u>. Here's how...

Formal Letters need Formal Language

<u>Formal</u> letters are to people you <u>don't know</u> very well. They are things like a letter of <u>complaint</u>, a letter <u>requesting information</u>, or a letter from your <u>headteacher</u> to your <u>parent</u>.

Q. Write a letter to a supermarket manager complaining about poor quality food you bought at their store.

Dear Sir/Madam,

I wish to inform you that I contracted food poisoning from a fish finger bought at your store. I purchased the item on Saturday March 14th and consumed it that night. It made me severely ill for several days.

Yours faithfully,

Osborn Outhouse (Mr.)

The letter uses <u>long words</u> and the tone is very <u>formal</u>.

If you start a formal letter "Dear <u>Sir/Madam</u>," always end with "Yours <u>faithfully</u>". If you know the <u>name</u> of the person you're writing to, use "Yours <u>sincerely</u>".

(In an <u>exam</u> these letters would be much <u>longer</u>.)

Informal Letters are Chatty

Letters to your <u>friends</u> are <u>informal</u>. You know your friends <u>well</u> — so you don't need to use formal language with them. Write in a <u>chatty</u> style, like you'd use if you were <u>talking</u> to them.

Q. Write a letter to a friend about something that happened to you recently.

The language is very <u>chatty</u> and <u>informal</u>. You wouldn't write this way to a stranger.

Dear Fred,

I've been feeling rotten these last few days. I ate a dodgy fish finger from the store. It whistled right through my system, I can tell you. I was throwing up all night. I'd steer well clear of them if I were you, mate.

See you soon,

Ossie

<u>Don't</u> end informal letters with "Yours faithfully" or "Yours sincerely". Write something like "<u>love</u>" or "<u>best wishes</u>" instead.

There's no need to give your <u>full</u> name — your friends know who you are.

A laid-back salad — informal lettuce...

If the question asks you to write a <u>letter</u>, stop and think about <u>who</u> the letter is to. <u>Don't</u> be <u>chatty</u> in a letter to someone you <u>don't know</u>, and don't be <u>formal</u> in a letter to a <u>friend</u>.

Revision Summary Questions

As if the reading part of your SATs wasn't enough, you've got to learn all this stuff about writing as well. Oh well — it has to be done. You wouldn't think there were so many tricks to doing something as simple as writing, but trust me — making sure you know all the stuff in this section will make a huge difference to the mark you get. Don't be a schmuck and think you can wing it. Go over this section till you can answer every last one of these questions.

1) How many writing questions do you have to do for the SAT?

2) What five things should you do as well as you can on the writing tasks?

3) What does it mean when the task says "you could write about..."?

4) Why are story questions often harder to do than you might think?

5) For the short question, should you:
   a) *ignore the bullet points*   b) *use a couple of them*   c) *use all of them?*

6) When should you decide what you should say in your answer?
   a) before you start writing it, in a plan.
   b) as you go along.
   c) over a cup of tea at home afterwards.

7) What type of answer _don't_ you need a plan for?
   a) Stories,
      b) Description pieces,
         c) Opinion questions,
            d) Ones you want to do badly on.

8) When you're writing about your opinions, when should you use your strongest point?

9) What should you make sure the style you write in matches?

10) How do you decide whether a letter is supposed to be formal or informal?

11) How do you end a formal letter when you know the name of the person you're writing to? And when you don't know their name?

12) In which type of letter should you use chatty language?

13) List a few ways you could end an informal letter.

That's not _quite_ what I meant...

Paragraphs

Paragraphs are a <u>big hassle</u>, but you get <u>more marks</u> for using them. Your writing's loads clearer when you use paragraphs — you need to know how to use 'em properly.

Always Use Paragraphs

Yes, you actually <u>get marks</u> for writing in paragraphs. The flip side is that you <u>lose marks</u> if you don't. It's not enough to use paragraphs <u>some</u> of the time — you need to use them <u>all</u> the time — in <u>stories</u> and <u>essays</u>.

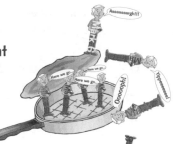

Paragraphs Make Things Clear

Crystal clear?

A paragraph is a group of sentences. These sentences talk about the same thing, or follow on from each other.

Every new paragraph must have a space between the margin and the first word.
Leave another space every time you start a new paragraph. This shows you're writing about something different.

Leave a little gap before the first word.

When you finish the last line of the paragraph, just stop.

Start a New Paragraph for Each Point in an Essay

Paragraphs help make your essay <u>clearer</u>.
A new paragraph shows that you're writing about <u>something new</u>.

This is a new point, so start a new paragraph.

The idea that school uniforms hide the difference between rich and poor is a fantasy. Everyone can tell whose uniform came from a discount store and whose came from a designer shop.
    Supporters of school uniform say that they don't want to turn school into a "fashion parade". In fact, this is exactly what they are doing when they point out the tiny ways in which a skirt or jumper doesn't quite fit the rules.

Stick to the point.

Applying to University — fill in a Uni-form...

Paragraphs — love 'em or hate 'em, you've got to use them. Start a <u>new paragraph</u> each and every time you start a new sentence with a brand <u>new</u> <u>idea</u>, or <u>angle</u>, or <u>argument</u>. Make it clear as day to everyone — especially the examiners — that you have a shiny new point to make.

Using Paragraphs

You need to know when to start a new paragraph — you can't guess. I know it's tough, but you'll have to learn the rules. Here's a nice golden rule to start with...

Here's the Golden Rule for Paragraphs

Start a new paragraph every time __something changes__.

When you Talk about a New Person

This paragraph is about Tanya.

> Tanya looked at the scene in despair. She couldn't believe that eight soldiers could make such a mess. She sighed and started to pick up the biscuits and crisps.
>
> A friendly face popped round the door. It was Brian. He watched Tanya grovelling around in the mess for a second or two before he spoke up.

I can't believe what a mess you've made.

This paragraph is about Brian.

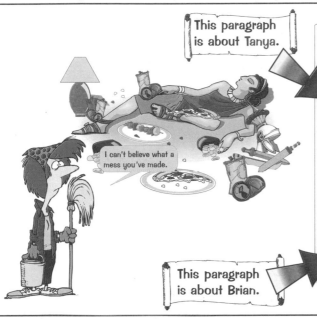

When Someone New Speaks

The same person is speaking here, so you don't need a new paragraph.

Someone new is speaking, so you need a new paragraph.

> "Please don't do that on your own, Tanya," said Brian. "Come on, I'll help you clear up," he offered.
> "Thanks, Brian, you're a star," replied Tanya appreciatively. "Where's everyone else? I thought there were five volunteers to clear up."
> "They're all dancing over there," he explained.

I'll help you clear up.

You're a star...

Using Paragraphs

Paragraphs are great. But there's no point in knowing that if you don't know when to use them. Here are <u>two more</u> times when you need to start a new paragraph.

A New Paragraph for a New Place...

> The shopping mall was utterly deserted. The uniformed security guards scratched their heads. What were they supposed to do now there was no-one to watch?
>
> Outside Bernie's gourmet chip shop in the High Street it was a rather different story. The crowd was three deep around the shop, all pushing and shoving to get to the door. "Give us battered rat!" they clamoured. "Give us rat on a stick!".

The story has moved to the chip shop, so this is a new paragraph.

No rats were harmed in the making of this page.

...or for a Different Time

This is talking about later that day.

This is talking about a long time afterwards.

> At last it was over. The voice called out again, "Are you alright?" I barely had the strength to answer. Relief flooded through me in a warm, drowsy wave. Soon I would be out of the cave and home.
>
> An hour later I was sitting in the coastguard's van, drinking hot tea from a flask. I could hear people talking all around me, but I couldn't really understand what they were saying. It was all a bit too much for me to take in. All I knew was that I was safe and everything was going to be alright.
>
> I don't think about my ordeal that much. When I look back, it seems like something that happened to somebody else. I can't believe that I could have been so reckless.

A herby fish dish — thyme and plaice...

Every time you <u>change time</u> or <u>place</u> in a <u>story</u>, a <u>letter</u> or an <u>essay</u> you have to use a new <u>paragraph</u>. No ifs, no buts — it's as simple as that. It's got to be <u>second nature</u> in the Exam.

Revision Summary Questions

Well, here we are at the end of another section, and what do you know, it's time for a set of revision summary questions. Remember, the point of these little jokers is to make sure that you've learnt something from the last three pages. Go through them, and don't you dare move on to the next section until you've got them all right. Ooh, I can be tough when I want to be...

1) What is a paragraph?

2) Do paragraphs make your writing *a)* clearer *b)* really complicated?

3) What should you do at the start of a paragraph?

4) What should you do at the end of the last line in a paragraph?

5) Do paragraphs make: *a)* not the blindest bit of difference to your mark

   b) a major difference to your mark   *c)* a nice accompaniment to steak and chips?

6) What is the golden rule for starting a new paragraph?

7) What's the rule when you're writing about new people?

8) What's the rule for when people are speaking?

9) Do you need to start a new paragraph when the same person carries on speaking?

10) What's the rule for changes of place?

11) What's the rule for changes of time? (you should be spotting some kind of pattern here...)

12) The following piece is really confusing. Turn it into a nice clear bit of writing by rewriting it with proper paragraphs:

    The biggest challenge facing junior league football today is the sheer number of red and yellow cards issued by referees. There is no doubt that standards of discipline have fallen sharply. Last year, 85 yellow cards and 14 red cards were issued in the first six weeks of the season. Already this year 136 yellow cards and 26 red cards have been issued. 4 players are facing a four-match ban. Hector Dalrymple, chairman of the UK federation of under-16 Football clubs, said last week that the situation was "reaching crisis point". Some, like Julian Fortescue of Edenhall School, disagree.

13) Write three paragraphs of a story, using the rules in this section.

14) Write a short essay about your school, using the rules in this section.

WRRRRRRRRRR

There's more than one way to divide writing into bite size chunks...

Basic Punctuation

This stuff is about as basic as it gets. People do get it wrong though — when they're <u>rushing</u> and not <u>thinking</u>. Learn it really well, and you won't even <u>need</u> to think about it.

Don't Lose Marks for Simple Stuff

Right, now this is stuff that you already know, but it doesn't hurt to go over it again.

Every sentence starts with a <u>capital letter</u>, and ends with a <u>full stop</u>.

This is the bit you have to think about more carefully.

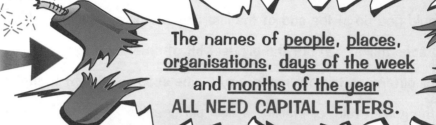

The names of <u>people</u>, <u>places</u>, <u>organisations</u>, <u>days of the week</u> and <u>months of the year</u> ALL NEED CAPITAL LETTERS.

<u>Y</u>ou haven't seen <u>B</u>en since <u>M</u>onday.

Capital letter   Capital letter   Full stop

<u>M</u>y aunt works in the marketing department of <u>A</u>ce <u>P</u>roducts.

Capital letter   Capital letters   Full stop

<u>W</u>e're going on holiday to <u>G</u>reece in <u>A</u>ugust.   Full stop

Capital letter   Capital letter   Capital letter

Questions need Question marks

If a sentence is a question it's got to have a question mark. Don't forget.

Boris, can you see Mrs Marple?

Only Use One Exclamation Mark

It was absolutely amazing! I couldn't believe I was really meeting Russian pop sensations, Steppes!!!!

 NO!

This makes your writing look silly, and you'll lose marks for it.

Getting this wrong — it's a capital crime...

OK, this is something that's <u>so basic</u> you'd only get it wrong if you weren't <u>awake</u>. What you have to do is make sure you <u>can</u> do it <u>in your sleep</u> — that way you won't make <u>daft mistakes</u>.

Sentences

Everything you write has to be in <u>proper sentences</u>, or you're just throwing away marks.

Every Sentence makes a Clear Point

A sentence that doesn't <u>make sense</u> isn't much use to anyone.

The Golden Rule
Every sentence must make sense on its own.

Don't let your Sentences Run on and on

Don't let your sentences all <u>run together</u> into a huge long mess.

We've run on too long...

The doorbell rang it was Theo he asked if I wanted a game of five-a-side.

This type of long messy sentence will <u>lose you marks</u>.

The doorbell rang. It was Theo. He asked if I wanted a game of five-a-side.

This sentence makes <u>one</u> point, and it's clear.

These sentences are short, but they're <u>proper sentences</u>.

A Sentence has to have a Verb

For a sentence to make sense, it has to be <u>about</u> something. It can only be <u>about</u> something <u>happening</u> if it's got a <u>verb</u>. Remember, <u>verbs</u> are <u>doing</u> and <u>being</u> words.

"Cost" is the verb.

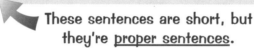

Barry bought a champion racing ram. It cost £2.50.

This is about him <u>buying</u> the ram.

This is about the ram <u>costing</u> £2.50.

Move it!

Barry bought a champion racing ram. For £2.50.

You can't do this. There's <u>no</u> verb, so this <u>isn't</u> a sentence.

A see-through pin — that's a clear point...

Working out when a sentence should <u>end</u> takes a little bit of <u>thought</u>. If you're <u>rushing</u> like crazy in the Exam, you'll <u>forget</u> about it. Keep your sentences <u>manageable</u> — don't let them turn into huge great gargantuan monsters. Remember this, too — no <u>verb</u>, no <u>sentence</u>.

Commas

Commas are horrible annoying little things. You're definitely going to need them in your writing Exam, so make sure you know how to use them.

Use Commas to Break up Sentences

If a sentence has more than one point, a comma keeps the points separate. Commas keep the items in lists separate, too.

I asked him to shut up, but he kept on yelling.

The comma keeps these two bits separate.

Commas add Extra bits to Sentences

After the match, we all went to Kathy's house for tea and toast.

Annie and Bert, who live next door, have built a bomb shelter.

The extra bit's in the middle of this sentence. The commas go around it like little brackets.

When you start a sentence with words like "Oh", "Right" or "Well", you need a comma to separate it from the rest of the sentence.

Now then, I think you need to lose that hat.

Well, I suppose you might just get away with it.

Don't Stick them in All Over the place

Don't just chuck me in!

The Mayor, Mrs Thribblewort, and the Treasurer, Mr Branchwood, said today, that the community centre would open on the 14th of September.

This comma's actually wrong — "said today" and "that the community centre..." go together — they're part of the same bit of info.

You should only put commas in when you want to break a sentence up into two bits or when you want to stick in a bit of extra information. Randomly throwing in a bunch of commas isn't going to work.

Blend in — be a comma chameleon...

Commas keep things apart in sentences. Make sure you use them to bracket off extra bits of information, but don't chuck them around willy-nilly. Learn the right way to use them.

Apostrophes

Lots of people mess this up — so get it learned. Make sure you know it <u>so</u> well that you'll <u>NEVER</u> forget it. When you've read it, cover the page and scribble down what's on it, then <u>check</u> you've got it right.

Use Apostrophes to show who Owns something

Mine, all mine!

Kulvinder's goldfish have all died.

When it's a group of people ending in s, add an <u>apostrophe</u>, but no <u>s</u>.

I washed the judges' wigs in soy sauce.

'Men', 'women' and 'children' follow the normal rule.

The women's race was cancelled.

Apostrophes are used in short forms of words

You need apostrophes for making <u>short</u> forms of words — like <u>we're</u> instead of <u>we are</u>.

I'm	he's	who's
I'd	won't	doesn't
I've	can't	here's
we'll	they're	we're

All of these need <u>apostrophes</u>. <u>Learn</u> them. Don't let the <u>easy</u> marks slip away.

Its and It's are Two Different Words

Getting <u>it's</u> and <u>its</u> mixed up is a mistake that people make all the time. They <u>are</u> confusing and they cause <u>more hassle</u> than anything else in English spelling. Get them <u>sorted out</u>.

The whale flipped <u>its</u> tail.

Its = <u>belonging</u> to it.

You <u>don't</u> use an apostrophe with <u>his</u> or <u>hers</u>, so <u>don't</u> use one with <u>its</u>.

<u>It's</u> thrown them into the air.

This is short for '<u>it has</u>'.

<u>It's</u> a long way down, captain.

This is short for '<u>it is</u>'.

An award for postmen — a post trophy...

Remember to put in your <u>apostrophes</u> or you can wave goodbye to a lot of marks. You really do have to <u>learn</u> the stuff about <u>its</u> and <u>it's</u>. Every time you use one of them, <u>think</u> about it.

Speech Marks

Speech marks do just what the name says — they show when someone's <u>speaking</u>.
All you've got to to do is use them in all the <u>right places</u>. You've guessed it — learn this page...

Speech Marks show when Someone is Speaking

Speech marks go at the
<u>start</u> of the speech...

... and speech marks go at
the <u>end</u> of the speech.

"These aren't my shoes," said Kevin.

You need <u>speech marks</u> because these are the words that Kevin <u>said</u>.

I won't ask Mary said.

This <u>isn't clear</u> without the speech marks...

...for a second, it looks like someone's saying that they won't ask Mary.

"I won't ask," Mary said.

You can <u>see</u> what's being <u>said</u> here.

When to Use Speech Marks

Be careful. You <u>don't</u> need speech marks if there's <u>no one talking</u> in your sentence.
Remember, though, <u>every time</u> someone <u>actually speaks</u> in a sentence, put speech marks.

NO SPEECH MARKS HERE

Tony said that he would lend Kevin a pair of trainers.

You <u>don't</u> need speech marks here.
No one's <u>actually</u> speaking.

SPEECH MARKS

Tony said, "I'll lend you a pair of trainers."

Look out! Someone <u>is</u> speaking in this sentence.
You need <u>speech marks</u> here, and don't you forget it.

Remember to always use speech marks when you <u>quote</u> from a piece of writing.
See Section 3 for stuff about quoting.

Speech Marks

Other bits of <u>punctuation</u> have to fit in with speech marks, too. <u>Learn</u> these two rules.

Start with a Capital Letter

"Don't leave the cage door open," warned Sally.

It <u>starts</u> with a <u>capital letter</u>.

Harry said, *"Don't worry, I won't."*

The spoken bit <u>always</u> starts with a capital letter, even if it isn't at the beginning of the sentence.

End with a Full Stop, a Comma or a Question Mark

Ruby said, *"I knew you shouldn't have trusted Harry."*

The sentence is finished, so you need a <u>full stop</u>.

"He doesn't know if he's coming or going," she declared.

The speech has finished <u>but</u> the sentence hasn't. You need a <u>comma</u> here, not a full stop.

"Had the bear been fed before it escaped?" asked Jill.

This is a question, so here's a <u>question mark</u>. Ace...

Don't forget — a <u>question</u> needs a <u>question mark</u>.

Speech marks — 10 out of 10 for a good 'un...

Don't **EVER** forget to put <u>speech marks</u> around something that a person's <u>actually saying</u>. The page on <u>punctuation</u> in speech marks is a bit harder, so make sure you <u>learn</u> the rules.

Revision Summary Questions

You have to pay attention to all the little bitty things like full stops and apostrophes. It's a major pain, but you've got to learn all this boring punctuation. It's no good being sort of vaguely aware of it. You have to know it back to front and inside out so that you don't make mistakes even when you're in a hurry. You don't want to be losing marks for getting the easy bits wrong. The only way to make sure you know it all is to go over these questions until you get every single one right.

1) What's wrong with this sentence?
   I've got tickets to see the raiders play the vikings on saturday.

2) What should you never do with exclamation marks?

3) What's the Golden Rule of Sentences?

4) Rewrite this as three proper sentences:
   I had to find out where the sound was coming from, as I walked closer I got more and more nervous, I wanted to scream, but nothing came out of my mouth.

5) Why isn't this a sentence? *Under a palm tree with a cool drink.* What's missing?

6) Are these proper sentences? If not, write a proper sentence instead:
   a) I enjoyed my holiday.   b) The sea was warm.   c) To the beach.

7) Put a comma in the right place to show there are two clear points here:
   Before I could warn him the General sat firmly down on the broken chair.

8) Put commas in the right places to show which is the extra information: *The masked mathematician her hair streaming out behind her hurtled towards the long division sum.*

9) My mate Flat Head doesn't bother learning punctuation.
   She just scatters commas through her writing and hopes.
   Will she: *a)* get most of them right?   *b)* make a bit of a mess of it?

10) What two things do apostrophes do?

11) What's the difference between its and it's?

12) Rewrite this properly: *This food mixer is brilliant. It's slicing attachment chops vegetables really quickly. Its got a separate liquidiser for soups and milk shakes.*

13) Put speech marks into these sentence:
    Earth has nothing better than a nice cosy armchair murmured Harry.

14) What's wrong with this sentence?
    The masked mathematician said "next week I can show you how the equation was solved"

Use Different Words

Writing 'properly' isn't enough — your writing has to be <u>interesting</u> too. A good way to start making your writing more interesting is to make sure you use lots of <u>different words</u>.

Use Different Words For The Same Thing

English has lots of words that mean the <u>same thing</u> as other words. That sounds a bit pointless. But it's actually <u>really handy</u>. Writing is very <u>dull</u> if it uses the same words all the time.

Have a look at these two pieces of writing and you'll see what I mean.

DULL

> I went to a nice Indian restaurant last night. The waiters were nice to us and the walls were painted in a nice shade of red. I had an onion bhaji to start with and it was really nice. Then I had a nice curry. After the meal the waiters brought us mints, which was nice of them.

It may be 'correctly' written and make perfect sense, but it's dead <u>boring</u> — the word 'nice' is in it again and again.

ACE

> I went to a great Indian restaurant last night. The waiters were friendly to us and the walls were painted in a lovely shade of red. I had an onion bhaji to start with and it was really tasty. Then I had a delicious curry. After the meal the waiters brought us mints, which was good of them.

Eek!
SAME WORD TRAP

This is <u>loads better</u>. It's exactly the same piece of writing except it uses lots of <u>different</u> words instead of "nice" — so seems more <u>interesting</u>.

It's easy to fall into the trap of using the same word all the time — especially <u>adjectives</u> like "<u>nice</u>" or "<u>weird</u>". You've got to keep an eye out and make sure you don't do it.

Look Out For Verbs As Well As Adjectives

It's not just with the adjectives that you can choose from oodles of different words.

Look at this little piece of writing. It becomes a lot more interesting just by using two <u>new verbs</u> instead of repeating "ran" twice.

> I ran to the post box with a letter, then I ran to the shop for some chocolate. After that I ran home so I wasn't late for tea.

> I ran to the post box with a letter, then I hurried to the shop for some chocolate. After that I raced home so I wasn't late for tea.

Here's another example:

You could say **Jump**

or **Leap**   or **Bound**

Think up <u>different</u> words whenever you can — they make your writing <u>tons better</u>.

Use Different Words

Examiners get dead impressed by a few <u>fancy words</u>. If you can <u>use</u> some in your SAT, they'll think you're real clever. And that means <u>better marks</u>.

Clever Words Impress The Examiner

Using <u>different</u> words is a good start. If you can use <u>different</u> and <u>clever</u> words, you're laughing teacakes. Long and clever words can really improve your SAT marks.

United played badly on Saturday. → *United played lamentably on Saturday.*

The pitch was in a poor condition. → *The pitch was in an atrocious condition.*

The referee made some very stupid decisions. → *The referee made some exceedingly moronic decisions.*

You can't use long fancy words <u>all</u> the time — that'd just sound <u>daft</u>. But you'll get extra marks if you throw them in <u>now and then</u>. So remember this rule:

sporadically   endeavour   substitute   concise

Every now and then, try to replace a short and simple word with a long and clever one.

elementary   complex   intellectual

That is a more advantageous compilation of phraseology.

Of course, you have to know some <u>clever words</u> before you can use them in your SATs. Get into the habit of <u>looking up</u> words you don't know in the <u>dictionary</u>. Chances are, the more words you know, the better you'll do.

Don't Worry (Too Much) About Spelling Long Words

Generally speaking, spelling is <u>really important</u>, and if you don't spell well you <u>WILL</u> lose marks for it.

BUT: examiners like long words so much that even if you get the spelling slightly wrong, you'll still get <u>credit</u> for trying. If you want to use a long word but you're not sure you know how to spell it, then <u>don't shy away</u>. Give it a go.

And one last thing — <u>DON'T</u> use a long word if you're <u>not sure</u> what it means.

Johnny, what is the definition of infelicitous?

IN-FELL-ICARUS

Use long words? — OK, wooooorrdddsssss...

You'll get much better marks if you make your writing <u>interesting</u>. The first step is to use <u>different</u> words, then throw in some <u>long</u> and <u>clever</u> words and hey presto — it'll be fascinating.

Don't Be Boring

Here are a couple more tricks that'll help you make your writing more interesting.

Don't use "And" and "Then" Too Much

This is something loads of people do, but it makes your writing a great big <u>yawn</u>.

> *I went to the beach and I put on my trunks and I walked to the sea and the water was warm and I swam for an hour.*

Great trunks...

> Instead of using "and" all the time, try to use commas and full stops.

> *I went to the beach, put on my trunks and walked to the sea. The water was warm. I swam for an hour.*

> It's **OK** to use "and" and "then" sometimes — but not too much.

> *We went to the bank then we had a coffee and then we went back to the car. Then we drove to the supermarket and did some shopping, then we drove home.*

> Changing the word order helps you not to use "then" all the time.

> *After going to the bank, we had a coffee. Then we went back to the car and drove to the supermarket. We did some shopping and drove home.*

Don't Start All Your Sentences The Same Way

This is another thing that makes your writing <u>dull</u> and <u>boring</u>. You'll <u>lose marks</u> if you do it in the SAT.

There was a chill in the air as Jo walked towards the house. There was nobody around. There was a big oak door and Jo knocked on it. There was a scream from inside the house.

> This says the same things, but in a more interesting way.

AAAHAHAHH

Mum's home early!

> *There was a chill in the air as Jo walked towards the house. Nobody was around. Jo knocked on the big oak door. A scream came from inside the house.*

Think of different ways to start your sentences.
It isn't all that hard, and it makes your writing a whole lot more <u>interesting</u> to read.

Don't Be Boring

Interesting writing doesn't only use different words, it uses <u>sentences</u> of <u>different lengths</u>.

Use a Variety of Short and Long Sentences

Sometimes a <u>short</u> sentence works best and sometimes a <u>long</u> one does. <u>Neither</u> of them work well <u>all</u> of the time. It's best to use a <u>variety</u> of different lengths.

The important thing to <u>remember</u> is not to write all short sentences, and not to write all long sentences. They both make your writing <u>boring</u>.

WOOF   WOOF **W O O F**

These chunks of writing are as dull as dishwater. That's because the sentences are all short or all long.

All short: DULL

I was walking to the station. I needed to catch a train. It left at one o'clock. I checked my watch. I was late. I decided to run. The streets were busy. I kept having to dodge people. That slowed me down. I came to a busy road. I had to wait for the green crossing sign. It seemed to take ages. Finally I crossed the road. I got to the station. The train hadn't left. It was only five to one. I looked at my watch again. It was fast.

All long: DULL

I was walking to the station because I needed to catch a train which left at one o'clock and I checked my watch and I was late so I decided to run but the streets were busy and I kept having to dodge people, which slowed me down. I came to a busy road where I had to wait for the green crossing sign and it seemed to take ages, but finally I crossed the road and got to the station where I saw the train hadn't left because it was only five to one so I looked at my watch again and it was fast.

LOADS MORE INTERESTING

Some short, some long:

I was walking to the station. I needed to catch a train which left at one o'clock. I checked my watch and I was late so I decided to run, but the streets were busy and I kept having to dodge people, which slowed me down. I came to a busy road where I had to wait for the green crossing sign. It seemed to take ages. Finally I crossed the road and got to the station, where I saw the train hadn't left because it was only five to one. I looked at my watch again. It was fast.

This is more like it. The mix of long and short sentences makes this version much more interesting to read.

Hmmm, looks a nice enough chap — a short sentence this time I think.

Make your writing more <u>interesting</u> — use sentences of different lengths.

Hunting wild pigs — nope, that'd be 'boaring'...

These things make your writing <u>boring</u>: using "<u>and</u>" and "<u>then</u>" too much, <u>starting</u> your sentences the <u>same way</u>, and using <u>all long</u> sentences or <u>all short</u> sentences. Just don't do it.

Adjectives

Adjectives are great for making your writing more <u>interesting</u>. Whenever you get a question asking you to "<u>describe</u>" something, make sure you <u>cram</u> your answer with adjectives.

Describe Things with Adjectives

<u>Adjectives</u> are describing <u>words</u>. They're a quick and easy way to <u>spice up</u> your writing.

Just <u>one</u> little adjective can completely change the <u>impression</u> you get from a sentence.

I ate a meal.   *I ate a delicious meal.*   *I ate a disgusting meal.*

And with <u>three</u> or <u>four</u> adjectives, you can really start to build up a picture.

I ate a delicious, sumptuous, lovingly-prepared meal.

I ate a disgusting, rancid, undercooked meal.

Who needs to cook it?...

Adjectives give you a Picture

Have a look at this piece of writing. It's the <u>adjectives</u> that really tell you what this <u>place is like</u>. Without them you <u>wouldn't</u> get much of an idea at all.

Gone Fishing.

Jordios is a quiet, sleepy village on the remote island of Toonos, forty miles from Athens. Miles of unspoilt, sandy beaches stretch along the deserted coastline. The air is thick with the sweet smell of pine trees, and you can sit in the shade of the tall, elegant cypress trees that grow all over the island.
Rickety wooden fishing boats set off every morning from the small, picturesque harbour. The fishermen's faces are gnarled and sunburnt. In the evenings the locals gather in the cosy, welcoming tavernas for a friendly chat over a refreshing glass of ouzo, and a game of table top bungee jumping.

Jug Suppliers — they give you pitchers...

Adjectives are a great way of <u>describing</u> things effectively. If you get a question in your SAT that asks you to <u>describe</u> something, using plenty of <u>adjectives</u> is the key to getting good marks.

Comparing

You need more to describe things than just plain old adjectives.
Another good way to describe something is to <u>compare</u> it to something else.

Less Than, More Than, The Least, The Most...

<u>Comparisons</u> are a great way to build up a <u>picture</u> of something. They sound <u>interesting</u> and they create a big <u>effect</u> in your reader's mind. They're also loads of <u>fun</u>.

Lisa felt sick. Her face went *green*. Lisa felt sick. Her face went *greener than an iceberg lettuce.*

It was *very cold*. It was *colder than an Arctic winter.*

He was *very bad* at beach volleyball. He was the *worst* beach volleyball player I had ever seen.

She was *beautiful*. She was the *most beautiful* woman this side of Stockport.

The key to making a good comparison is to pick something <u>sensible</u>. It's no good saying "it was colder than a pair of scissors", or "Lisa's face went as green as a doorbell".

Careful — Don't Write "More Better"

There's one <u>mistake</u> that tons of people make but which will <u>lose</u> you loads of marks.

When you're making a comparison, you must <u>EITHER</u> say "more ... than" or "the most...", <u>OR</u> you use the form of the word that ends in "er" or "est". You DON'T do BOTH.

Ted is the *cleverest* boy in school.
NOT the "most cleverest".

You are the *most sporty* person I know.
NOT the "most sportiest".

Suzanne is *prettier than* her sister.
NOT "more prettier".

You are *more intelligent than* a brick.
NOT "more intelligenter".

This rented house is the smallest — it's 'leased'...

<u>Comparisons</u> are another top way of making your writing more <u>interesting</u> — examiners love them. But don't get confused — you <u>either</u> use more/most, <u>or</u> you use the er/est ending. Not both.

More Comparing

You don't have to use "<u>more than</u>" or "<u>less than</u>" when you're making comparisons.
Another way of doing it is to say one thing is <u>like</u> another. That can be really <u>effective</u> too.

Say that One Thing is Like Another

There are <u>two</u> ways of doing this.

① The first is to take an <u>adjective</u>, think of a <u>comparison</u>, and then instead of using "more" and "than", you use "<u>as</u>" and "<u>as</u>".
You do it like this:

Anyone for Mud-Pool?

Beth felt *as* happy *as* a hippo in a mud pool.

That idea was *as* useless *as* a chocolate teapot.

Chocolate teapot — doesn't seem like such a bad idea to me.

② The other way of saying one thing is <u>like</u> another is nice and simple — you use the word "<u>like</u>".

Look, a chocolate teapot, ace.

Her eyes lit up *like* the sky on bonfire night.

I'd forgotten my gloves and soon my fingers were *like* blocks of ice.

It's Okay to Exaggerate to Make an Effect

Don't worry about <u>exaggerating</u> when you make a comparison. That's why it's so much <u>fun</u>.

Jack was *as* tall *as* a tree.

Freda was *as* old *as* the hills.

EXCLUSIVE Why I Lied About My Height

Trees are generally pretty tall, and hills are pretty old, so these are <u>good comparisons</u> to use.
You don't <u>literally</u> mean that Jack was as tall as a tree or
Freda was as old as a hill — but people will understand.

(If your comparisons had to be totally <u>accurate</u>, there'd be no point. You'd have to write stuff like "Jack was as tall as a six foot two inch tree", or "Freda was as old as a ninety-eight year old hill".)

I've told you a million times — stop exaggerating...

Remember the <u>two</u> ways to say that one thing is <u>similar</u> to another — use "<u>as ... as</u>" or use the word "<u>like</u>". It's OK to <u>exaggerate</u> when you make comparisons — that's what makes them <u>interesting</u>.

Speaking Figuratively

If you speak "literally", you mean exactly what you say. Saying something you don't literally mean is called speaking figuratively. We all do it — and it can really liven up your writing.

Say Things you don't Literally mean

When you speak figuratively, you talk about one thing as if it <u>is</u> something else.

This is another way of making a <u>comparison</u>. Instead of saying that one thing is <u>like</u> another thing, you talk about the first thing as if it <u>actually</u> is the other thing that you're comparing it to.

> Bob cried so hard that a river flowed down his cheeks.

> Sarah needed a glass of water — there was a desert in her mouth.

There wasn't <u>literally</u> a river flowing down Bob's cheeks, or a desert in Sarah's mouth.

This is a clever way of saying that Bob's tears were <u>like</u> a river, and Sarah's mouth was <u>as dry as</u> a desert.

Sometimes when you speak figuratively it seems to have <u>nothing at all</u> to do with what you actually mean — but it's <u>obvious</u> when you think about it.

> Dog Girl tried to delete the old files from her computer, but she wiped the entire hard drive by mistake. She had thrown the baby out with the bathwater.

Dog Girl <u>hadn't</u> actually gone near any <u>real</u> babies. This is just a figurative way of saying that in the process of throwing away <u>something</u> she <u>didn't</u> need, she got rid of something very <u>important</u> as well.

Don't Use Too Many Clichés — they Get Boring

Some figures of speech are used so often that they become <u>boring</u>. They're called <u>clichés</u>. You hear them a lot when people are talking about sport.

> I'm as sick as a parrot.

> The atmosphere's electric.

> It isn't over till the fat lady sings.

Well, I'm a fat electric singing parrot, that's NOT a cliché

You can get away with using <u>some</u> clichés in your SAT, but don't use <u>too</u> many — the examiner will think you haven't got anything <u>original</u> to say.

He said, "Speak figuratively," — I said, "5738492"...

Speaking figuratively means talking about one thing <u>as if it's something else</u>, and it's a great way to spice up your writing. Careful, though — don't use too many clichés. Be <u>original</u> if you can.

Revision Summary Questions

So now you know loads of tricks to help you make your writing interesting. It's important that you learn all this and remember to use it in the SAT writing questions. Imagine you're the examiner — if you've got to read something that's dull and boring, you're not going to give it many marks. But interesting writing isn't something you can do just like that — you have to practise it so it becomes natural. Make sure you can answer all these questions, and every time you write something, try to put what you've learned into action.

1) Is using the same word all the time: *a)* nice *b)* nice *c)* nice *d)* incredibly boring?

2) Is the examiner going to be impressed by someone who can use clever words correctly?

3) Should you aim to use long and clever words:
   a) never *b)* all the time *c)* every now and then, but only when you know the meaning?

4) When you read a word and you don't know what it means, what should you do?

5) If you're in your SAT and you know a long and clever word that'd be really appropriate for something you're writing, but you're not 100% sure how to spell it, what should you do?

6) Which two words do you have to watch out for using too much?
   a) "and" and "then".
   b) "endogenous" and "exogenous".
   c) "Manchester" and "United".

7) Why is it a bad idea to start all your sentences the same way?

8) What do judges and SAT students have in common?
   a) they have to wear silly wigs.   *b)* they should try to use sentences of varying lengths.

9) Why are adjectives great?
   a) they make you a cup of tea in the morning.
   b) they help you to describe something.
   c) you can cuddle them and take them for walks and stuff.

10) Which of these comparisons works better?
   a) It was hotter than the Sahara Desert.   *b)* It was hotter than a piece of string.

11) Why?

12) Which of these comparisons works better?
   a) It was brighter than a candle.   *b)* It was brighter than a million suns.

13) Why?

14) Which of these is wrong?
   a) You're weirder than me. *b)* She's my bestest friend. *c)* He's more insane, though.
   d) I'm the most funniest. *e)* We're the most charming. *f)* They're much more better.

15) What are two ways of saying that one thing is similar to another?

16) Is it OK to exaggerate when you're making comparisons?

17) What's the difference between speaking figuratively and speaking literally?

18) When is it OK to use clichés?
   a) Now and again.
   b) Most of the time.
   c) Till the cows come home.

That's an interesting 'IT'...

Persuading

Sometimes you'll get a question in your SAT that asks you to write about <u>your opinions</u> — like in a <u>speech</u> or a <u>newspaper column</u>. That means you have to <u>write persuasively</u>.

Persuasive Writing is Like Selling Something

Persuasive writing is all about <u>making someone else agree</u> with your point of view.
Trying to persuade someone to agree with you is exactly like trying to <u>sell</u> a product.

You need to sound <u>positive and certain</u> that you're right.
If you're <u>half-hearted</u> and wishy-washy about what you're saying, no one is going to be <u>convinced</u>.

Make sure you've got enough good reasons to <u>back up your opinion</u>.

You'll also need some <u>handy tricks</u> for presenting those opinions. <u>Here they are</u>.

Work Out the Opposite View — Then Say It's Wrong

A good way to start is to look at it from <u>the other point of view</u>. Think about why people might <u>not</u> agree with you — then you can work out how to <u>prove them wrong</u>.

Here's how you might plan a speech trying to <u>persuade</u> people to <u>support</u> a <u>ban</u> on foxhunting.

Notes: Reasons why people disagree with banning foxhunting
1. Countryside jobs — but there aren't that many
2. Need to cull foxes — but there are more humane ways
3. Tradition — but so were bear-baiting and witch-burning

These are reasons it should **NOT** be banned.

Here's how you can say these reasons are <u>wrong</u>.

And here's how you could write out one of those points.

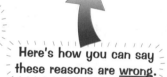

Why Foxhunting Should Be Banned
Supporters of foxhunting say that it's a tradition. But in the past, it was traditional to burn witches and bait bears. Times change, and society moves on. Just because something is traditional is no reason to keep it.

Show that you've <u>thought</u> about what your opponents say and you still <u>disagree</u> with them.
You'll have more chance of <u>persuading</u> other people that your <u>own</u> view is <u>right</u>.

Hit me with a wallet till I give in — 'purse'uasive...

Persuasive writing is all about <u>selling your point of view</u> to other people. A good way to start is to ask yourself what the <u>opposite arguments</u> are, write them down, and then say why they're <u>wrong</u>.

Exaggerating

When you're trying to <u>persuade</u> people to agree with you, it's a good idea to make your <u>own</u> points sound even <u>better</u> than they are, and your <u>opponents'</u> points seem <u>even worse</u>.

Exaggerate Your Good Points

This is a <u>great</u> point.

It might sound a bit <u>unfair</u> to exaggerate how good your own arguments are. But <u>don't worry</u> — everyone does it. If you don't exaggerate, people will actually think your points are <u>weak</u>.

If you have a point worth making — do it with style.

Version 1 — Rubbish:

> Global warming could be <u>quite</u> a problem. <u>Some scientists</u> think the earth is getting warmer quite quickly. That <u>might mean</u> that <u>a fair bit</u> of farmland turns into desert, so <u>people</u> might <u>not have enough food</u>.

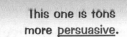
This one is tons more <u>persuasive</u>.

It uses <u>strong</u> words like as "<u>massive</u>", "<u>frightening</u>" and "<u>huge</u>" instead of <u>weak</u> ones like "<u>quite</u>" or "<u>a fair bit</u>".

It says "<u>many</u> scientists" instead of "some".

It says "<u>will</u>" and "<u>huge areas</u>" instead of "might" and "a fair bit"

It talks about "<u>billions</u> of people" instead of just saying "people".

It uses the <u>scary</u> word "<u>starve</u>" instead of "not have enough food".

Version 2 — Good:

> Global warming is a <u>massive</u> threat to the very future of humanity. <u>Many scientists</u> believe the earth is getting warmer at a <u>frightening</u> rate. If this continues, <u>huge</u> areas of farmland <u>will</u> turn into desert, causing <u>billions of people</u> to <u>starve</u>.

Be careful, though — you're allowed to exaggerate, but you're <u>not</u> allowed to <u>lie</u>. You <u>can't</u> say things that <u>aren't true</u>, like "global warming will cause aliens to take over the Earth".

If you say things that <u>obviously aren't true</u>, people won't trust the rest of your arguments.

Make Your Opponents Sound Crazy

Putting your opponents' point of view in your own words is a good way of making them sound bad.

You can also <u>exaggerate</u> what people who disagree say, to make them sound <u>crazy</u>.

> Some businessmen believe we have no responsibility to the environment. They think it doesn't matter if we keep on churning out deadly greenhouse gases. All they care about is making profits.

You can be <u>harsh</u> — as long as you don't <u>tell any actual lies</u>.

10 out of 10 for exagge — a high exagge-rating...

Exaggeration is a <u>crucial trick</u> for good persuasive writing. You can use it to make <u>yourself</u> sound <u>good</u>, and make your <u>opponents</u> sound <u>bad</u>. But make sure you <u>don't lie</u>. That's all there is to it.

Persuasive Tricks

Here are three nifty tricks which will make your persuasive writing a whole load better.

Talk About "We" and "Us" Whenever You Can

Surely we all agree that what's best for us is to give me the cake?

If you want someone to agree with you, it's a good idea to make them think they have a lot in common with you.

Using the words "we" and "us" is a sneaky way to make your audience feel like they ought to be on your side.

Surely we all agree that cruelty to animals is wrong.

These are much better than "I think that cruelty..." or "...that affects some people" would be.

Pollution is an issue that affects all of us.

Use Questions To Make Your Points

Asking people something is a great way to make them sit up and take notice — even though you don't want an answer.

The trick is to say the question so that there can only be one possible answer.

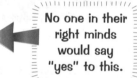

Does anyone really want to live in a world without clean air to breathe?

No one in their right minds would say "yes" to this.

Alternatively, you can ask a question then go on to answer it yourself.

And why doesn't the government do anything about it? I'll tell you why. It's because they want big businesses to give them donations.

Use "Magic Threes" — Three Adjectives

Three is a magic number when you're writing persuasively. If you use three adjectives to describe something, it sounds much more effective than only using one or two.

THREE

Fossil fuels are dirty, dangerous and outdated.

Renewable energy is clean, safe and efficient.

Lorries that make you agree — persuasive trucks...

Talk about "we" and "us", use questions to make your points, and use adjectives in groups of three. These are great tricks — listen to politicians' speeches and you'll hear them all the time.

Don't Be Rude

Even if you're <u>really convinced</u> about something, you're not going to <u>persuade</u> anyone by being <u>rude</u>. People will <u>only</u> want to listen to what you say if you're <u>polite</u>.

Keep Your Writing Polite

If they don't agree with you, being <u>rude</u> to them isn't going to help. It'll just get their backs up.

Recycling is very important. Anybody who doesn't recycle their waste is stupid and selfish.

NO! People will be put off and stop listening

Much better. People will listen and you might change their minds.

No matter how strongly you feel about something, <u>always</u> be <u>polite</u>.

Recycling is very important. It's something every one of us can do to help our planet.

Keep Criticisms General And Impersonal

Don't make <u>direct attacks</u> on your <u>opponents</u>. It'll make you sound angry and <u>aggressive</u>, and anyone who's <u>neutral</u> will be <u>turned off by your attitude</u>. And that includes the examiner.

If you think monkey juggling is acceptable, I think you're wrong.

Instead of this, say this...

Some people think monkey juggling is acceptable, but I think they're wrong.

...or better still, this.

It is sometimes said that monkey juggling is acceptable, but I think that's wrong.

Who's juggling WHAT?

Make Your Positive Points Personal

...But for <u>positive points</u>, be <u>as personal as you like</u>. Using "<u>you</u>" gets your audience to sit up and listen, and using "<u>we</u>" makes them think they're <u>on your side</u>.

You can make a difference by not buying this company's products. Together we can bring this awful practice to an end.

This sort of <u>personal</u> language is especially <u>effective</u> when you use it as an ending.

Don't make a rude-imentary mistake...

Always remember to <u>be polite</u> in your persuasive writing, and make your <u>negative</u> points <u>impersonal</u>. Being <u>rude and aggressive</u> rubs people up the <u>wrong way</u> — and it'll lose you marks.

Revision Summary Questions

This is the last section about the writing section of your SAT, and the last section of the whole book (Woo Hoo!) — just think if you've learned everything in the book so far, you'll have learned all the skills you need to get through the SAT. But before you can say that, you have to make sure you know this section properly. It's well worth it because chances are you'll get a question in the SAT that wants you to write persuasively — whether it's a speech, a magazine article or a letter. And persuasive writing is something you can get really good at just by learning the tricks in these pages.

1) What should you do after you have listed the reasons why people might disagree with you?

2) How can you make your opponents' beliefs sound crazy?

3) Which of these is a good use of exaggeration?
   a) "The arms industry causes some suffering in the world".
   b) "The arms industry is directly responsible for causing untold misery to millions".
   c) "The arms industry likes to kidnap newborn babies and roast them on a spit".
   What is wrong with the other two sentences?

4) If I said it was a good idea to tell lies about your opponents, would I be right?

5) Why is it a good idea to use "we" and "us" a lot in persuasive writing?

6) Which of these would be a good question to use in a piece of persuasive writing?
   a) "What is the capital of Estonia?"
   b) "Would you like your children to grow up in a world without wild flowers?"
   c) "Can anyone lend me a fiver?"

7) What makes it such an effective question?

8) What's the other good trick to use with questions?

9) Is the idea of using three adjectives to describe something:
   a) daft.
   b) pointless and strange.
   c) clever, valuable and effective?

10) What would you write to try to convince someone who thinks that you should be rude in persuasive writing that it's better to be polite?
   a) "Don't be idiotic, you pea-brained fool, that idea stinks."
   b) "Many people find that being polite works much better."

11) Why is it a good idea to keep your criticisms general and impersonal?

12) Can your positive points be personal?

13) What is an especially effective time to use personal language?
   a) As an ending.
   b) Eight o'clock, but ten o'clock on Thursdays and Fridays.
   c) When asking to borrow a fiver.

So, what's so great about purse-wading again?

Index

Index